# Haunted Castles

Mark Ronson

Beaver Books

First published in 1982 by
The Hamlyn Publishing Group Limited
London · New York · Sydney · Toronto
Astronaut House, Feltham, Middlesex, England

© Copyright Text Mark Ronson 1982
© Copyright Illustrations
The Hamlyn Publishing Group Limited 1982
Chapter openers by Michael Jackson
ISBN 0 600 20481 2

Reproduced, printed and bound in Great Britain by
Hazell Watson & Viney Ltd, Aylesbury, Bucks

*For Paul Alexander*

# *Contents*

# Acknowledgements

The photographs in the insert are the copyright of the following people and are reproduced with their kind permission:

page 1 Tower of London, Ministry of Public Building and Works

page 2 top, Windsor Castle, G. F. Allen; bottom, Hermitage Castle, Hamlyn Group Picture Library

page 3 top, Glamis Castle, M. W. Elphinstone; bottom, Corfe Castle, Albert Kerr

page 4 top, Berkeley Castle, Hamlyn Group Picture Library; bottom, Camelot, Bibliothèque Royale Albert Premier

page 5 top, Rosslyn Castle, *The Scotsman and Evening Despatch*; bottom, Caerphilly Castle, British Tourist Authority

page 6 top, Bamburgh Castle, Bertram Unne; bottom, Herstmonceux Castle, Noel Habgood

page 7 Dover Castle, British Tourist Authority

page 8 Warwick Castle, British Tourist Authority

# Introduction

One survey puts the number of reported hauntings in the United Kingdom at ten thousand. Supernatural sites range from modern council houses to old churches and abbeys, but, as one would expect, our oldest and grandest ghosts inhabit castles. This is because they are our most ancient buildings, all have seen their share of dark deeds, and from the time of the prehistoric hillfort up to the Civil War, castles dominated the lives of the people. After the hillforts came the great Roman castles, and after them the massive frowning fortresses built by the Normans to control the country.

As time passed the people frequently found castles to be places of refuge in times of trouble, and the baron's knights and men-at-arms often became the peasants' only protection against outlaw bands. But in times of civil war or when the king's rule broke down, masters of castles could behave in any way they wished. The results were sometimes terrible, as in the strife-ridden reign of King Stephen when, according to the *Anglo-Saxon Chronicle*:

> Every powerful man built his castles and held them against him [the king] and they filled the country full of castles. . . . When the castles were built they filled them with devils and with wicked men. Then both by night and by day they took those people they thought had any goods, both men and women, put them in prison and tortured them with indescribable torture to extort gold and silver. No martyrs were ever tortured as they were. They hung by the thumbs or by the heads and corslets were hung on their feet. Knotted ropes were put round their heads and twisted till they penetrated to the brain. I have neither the ability nor the power to tell all the horrors or all the torments then inflicted upon the wretched people in this country.

But it must be remembered that castles were not only fortresses and prisons – they were also homes, which is why there are so many lady phantoms. Typical of these is the Green Lady of Crathes Castle near Aberdeen. This ghost was seen to glide across a certain room before a death occurred in the Burnett family who owned the castle for centuries. Each time she appeared she crossed the floor to an ancient carved fireplace where she lifted up a phantom child, after which the pair would melt away. At last workmen renovating the castle removed the hearth of this fireplace, and found beneath it the skeleton of a woman with a baby's skeleton in her arms. . . .

Some hauntings are much more bizarre. Dunphail Castle near Forres in Grampian Region boasts one of the most frightening, in the form of five spectral heads. The story goes back to when the castle was besieged by the Earl of Moray. The inhabitants were faced with starvation and on one moonless night five men slipped out through the postern gate. Some time later they returned with sacks of meal which they threw over the wall before going away for more. When they came back a second time they were captured by Moray's retainers and beheaded, after which their bloodied heads were hurled over the ramparts with the mocking taunt of 'Here's beef for your bannocks!' – a bannock being an unleavened cake made from barley meal.

You will find that the amount of information available about castles and their ghosts varies greatly, and if you go visiting haunted castles you will also find great differences in their appearance. Some are in splendid condition, often a cross between a stately home and a museum, others are just ruins on remote windswept sites, yet all have their magic and are worth exploring. At the end of the book there is information about visiting haunted castles and, while I cannot guarantee that you will see a ghost, at least you will know where to look.

*Mark Ronson*

## Chapter 1

# The Terrible Tower

If you live in London you are within a bus or Underground ride of one of the most haunted places in the land – the Tower of London. About nine hundred years ago William the Conqueror had Caen stone brought from France to build it because he did not trust the 'fierce populace' of London. Since then it has been used as a royal palace, a fortress, a prison and even a zoo. And each aspect has left behind its own particular ghosts.

Much new building went on at the Tower during the reign of Henry III, and to improve its appearance the castle was whitewashed in 1240, an event commemorated in the name of the White Tower. A few years afterwards a building was erected to house an elephant which was a gift from the King of France and which must have filled Londoners with amazement.

From then on the castle was frequently added to until it reached the shape and covered the area of more than seven hectares which we know today. Near the causeway over the moat, built in 1278 by Edward I and still the means by which we enter the Tower, a zoo was kept in the Lion Tower, though both have long since disappeared.

Over a considerable period of the Tower of London's history members of royalty as well as rebellious nobles and commoners have been put to death or made to suffer

7

behind its massive walls. After dark, when the tourists have gone home and the famous ravens are asleep in their cage by the Lanthorn Tower, such phantoms as Edward V and his brother, Queen Anne Boleyn, Lady Jane Grey, Sir Walter Raleigh and Guy Fawkes have materialised, sometimes with terrifying effect.

The chapel of St Peter ad Vincula, meaning St Peter in Chains', is the best place to begin a ghost tour of the Tower. It was used as the burial place for the more important prisoners who were executed on Tower Hill and Tower Green, and has been described as 'the saddest spot in Christendom'. In 1876 Queen Victoria became interested in the gloomy old church and ordered the floor to be taken up so that the remains of human bodies beneath it could be given proper burial. Workmen removed the stone flags and found over two hundred skeletons. One of these, a 'woman of excessively delicate proportions', was thought to be Anne Boleyn, who had been beheaded by command of her husband Henry VIII.

On 19 May 1536 she was led out to Tower Green before which the principal nobles and aldermen of London were waiting. Calmly she ascended the scaffold and her head was then struck from her body with a sword wielded by a headsman brought over specially from Calais. Execution by the sword was a French custom which up to then had not been practised in England.

The day after the execution Henry married Jane Seymour.

The body of Anne was buried in St Peter ad Vincula, and it is to this church that her spirit sometimes returns. One night an officer making a tour of inspection saw a light showing behind its clear windows. He asked a sentry what was the cause. The soldier told him that he did not know but that he had often noticed it.

The officer was so intrigued that, being unable to enter the locked church, he propped a ladder against the wall, climbed up and looked in through a window. He

8

saw a number of people in old-fashioned costumes walking in mournful procession down the aisle. In front was a woman who, although her head was averted, resembled portraits of Anne Boleyn which the officer had seen. The phantom promenade continued up and down for several minutes, then the figures vanished, and the church was filled with its normal darkness.

Anne Boleyn is also reported to haunt Tower Green, for she was one of the seven prisoners who were given the privilege of being executed there instead of providing a spectacle for the London mob on Tower Hill. Sometimes she has been seen walking to the White Tower, at other times only her footsteps are heard.

The reality of this haunting can be gauged from a strange incident which occurred in 1864. A soldier from the King's Royal Rifle Corps was found lying unconscious beside his sentry box by what was then called the King's House and is now known as the Queen's House. To be asleep or drunk while on guard duty is obviously one of the worst military offences, and the man was brought before a court martial.

He told the tribunal that he had seen a white figure approaching out of the gloom. He had shouted a challenge the three prescribed times, and as the stranger still advanced, he raised his rifle . . . and then saw that the form before him was a headless woman. The shock was such that he fainted.

Two other witnesses gave evidence in support of his story and the court was so impressed by their sincerity that he was acquitted.

The soldier was luckier than a sentry who was on guard at the Jewel House one midnight in January 1816. Then he saw a figure like a huge bear rearing up at the door of the regalia room. He raised his musket and lunged at the animal with his bayonet, with the result that the weapon passed through the spectral beast and the point struck the door, making an indentation in the wood. The bear advanced menacingly on the soldier

9

who was so terrified that he collapsed on the stone floor in a faint. Hearing the noise, other sentries ran to the spot, and the unconscious man was carried to the guard-room.

Edmund Swifte, who had been appointed Keeper of the Crown Jewels two years earlier, visited the guard, who was in bed with shock, and wrote down his account of what had happened. Another sentry gave evidence that he had spoken to the victim just before the alarm had been raised, and that he had been alert and sober.

In his account, Mr Swifte wrote: 'I saw him once again on the following day, but changed beyond my recognition, in another day or two the brave and steady soldier, who would have mounted a breach or led a forlorn hope with unshaken nerves, died at the presence of a shadow.'

If you are wondering why a bear should haunt the Tower of London, the answer may be in the fact that for a long time it contained a zoo which had been established by Henry III and it was recorded in an old chronicle that the king had a pet bear which used to catch fish in the Thames, probably a polar bear given him by the King of Norway. If it was not the spectre of this animal, it might have been a victim of the brutal sport of bear-baiting which lasted into the middle of last century when it was made illegal.

The two most pathetic phantoms in the Tower of London are those of boys who died for no other reason than that they had royal blood in their veins. These are the ghosts of Edward V and his younger brother Richard – the tragic Princes in the Tower – who have been seen at various times over the last five centuries in the Bloody Tower where tradition tells that their uncle Richard III was responsible for having them smothered with pillows.

Unfortunately these two pale spectres have not been able to give any clue as to one of the greatest mysteries in English history – what their real fate was. Since Tudor times King Richard has been blamed for their deaths, yet the evidence against him was given verbally by Henry Tudor nearly two decades after he had usurped Richard's throne, and these spoken words, without a shred of documentary evidence, are the only explanation of young Edward's disappearance.

According to King Henry, Sir James Tyrrell, who had been executed in the Tower and was safely out of the way, had confessed to arranging the murder of the little princes on behalf of Richard III. They were to be done to death in their room in the Bloody Tower by a groom called John Dighton, a known murderer Miles Forest and the gaoler with the sinister name of Black Will Slaughter.

According to an old account:

This Miles Forest and John Dighton about midnight (the seelie children lieing in their beds) came into the chamber and suddenlie lapping them amongst the clothes, so bewarpped them and entangled them, keeping downe by force the feather-bed and pillowes hard unto their mouths, that within a while, smothered and stifled, their breaths failing, they gave up to God their innocente soules.

Yet if King Richard was responsible, it seems strange that the mother of the little princes was on friendly terms with him until his death on Bosworth Field, her daughters often being guests at his palace for court festivities after their brothers were supposed to have been murdered. It could be that they met their fate after the Tudors had replaced the Plantagenets.

When excavations were being carried out in 1674 workmen found two skeletons under the foundations of a staircase in the Tower. Believing them to be the remains of Edward V and his brother, Charles II commissioned Sir Christopher Wren to design a tomb for 'the supposed bodies of the two princes' which would be built in Westminster Abbey. (They were the third set of bones which had been found in the Tower and attributed to the little princes.)

In 1933 a Professor Wright opened the marble tomb and after examining the bones declared them to be the skeletons of two children aged twelve and a half and ten years. Nothing else could be deduced from them and those who hoped the tomb contained a clue to the mystery of Edward V were disappointed.

And the spirits in the Bloody Tower remain mute.

Another victim whose only crime was to have royal blood was Lady Jane Grey – 'queen for a day', though in fact her tragic reign lasted for nine days. A cousin of the young king Edward VI, she was the daughter of Henry Grey, the Duke of Suffolk. A remarkably clever girl, she was forced at the age of fifteen to marry Guildford Dudley, the son of the scheming Duke of Northumberland. The wedding took place on 21 May 1553, and the duke was delighted because he saw Guildford winning the throne through Jane's royal connections.

At the time of the wedding King Edward, who had no child to inherit his crown, agreed to make any male children that Jane should have in the future heirs to the throne. Edward died a few weeks later, and Guildford Dudley lost no time in taking his wife before the Council and claiming that she had been named by the late king as his successor – a lie which he backed up with forged evidence.

The Council accepted this and, four days after the death of the king, Jane was taken down the Thames by barge to the Tower of London where she was proclaimed as the new queen.

At the same time Princess Mary – later to be known as 'Bloody Mary' – claimed that as half-sister to Edward VI she was the rightful heir. But the Council still regarded Jane as the true queen and the Crown Jewels were presented to her by the Lord Treasurer.

Guildford Dudley tried to force Jane to make him king, but although she was only a puppet in the political intriguing, she bravely refused, saying that only Parliament could do so.

Princess Mary rallied her supporters at Framlingham Castle, then with over twelve thousand followers marched on London where the citizens hailed her as queen. In one of the worst acts of betrayal in English history, Jane's cowardly father, in an effort to save himself, publicly proclaimed Mary queen at the Tower gates and informed his daughter that she was now a prisoner of the new queen.

His treachery was rewarded with a pardon and Jane was confined to the home of the Yeoman Gaoler. She was found guilty of treason, which carried the death penalty, but it was thought this was a mere formality and that she would soon be allowed to retire into private life. But her father, changing sides again, became involved in a plot against Mary, and the queen, fearing that Jane would be used to rally people in rebellion against her, let the death sentence stand.

The executions of Jane and her over-ambitious husband took place in February 1554.

Guildford Dudley was taken to be beheaded on Tower Hill. Jane watched him go from a window and saw his headless body brought back to be buried in St Peter ad Vincula. Then it was her turn to be taken to a scaffold especially erected for her on Tower Green to save her from the jeers of the crowd. A handkerchief was bound round her head, and blindfolded she was unable to locate the headsman's block.

'What shall I do?' she asked pathetically as she groped for it. 'Where is it?'

Since that sad day the ghost of Lady Jane Grey has been seen close to the chapel where she was buried, her last recorded appearance being on the Salt Tower in 1957.

Jane's father gained nothing by his political intrigues.

After his conspiracy against Queen Mary, he fled to Astley Castle in Warwickshire, where he remained hidden until he was given up by his park-keeper and suffered the same death as his daughter. In 1849 his head was discovered in a church in the London street called the Minories, several cuts on the neck showing the executioner's lack of skill.

Astley Castle, which is now a hotel, was haunted by Suffolk's headless phantom for many years.

To me the strangest story connected with the Tower of London was written down by Mr Swifte, the Keeper of the Crown Jewels who described the death of the sentry. It reads more like a piece of science fiction than a ghost story, and to this day there has been no explanation for what he saw one Saturday night in October 1817.

I was at supper with my wife, our little boy and my sister-in-law, in the Jewel House, which then, comparatively modernised, is said to have been the doleful prison of Anne Boleyn.

The room was irregularly shaped, having three doors and two windows, which last are cut nearly nine feet [three metres] deep into the outer wall. Between these is a chimney-piece projecting far into the room, which then was surmounted by a large oil picture.

On the evening in question, the doors were all closed and dark cloth curtains were let down over the windows, the only light in the room being that from two candles placed on the table. I sat at the foot of the table, with my son on my right hand, his mother fronting the chimney-piece and her sister on the opposite side.

'I had offered a glass of wine and water to my wife, when on putting it to her lips she paused and exclaimed: 'Good God! What is that?' I looked up and saw a cylindrical figure like a glass tube, seemingly about the thickness of my arm, hovering between the

14

ceiling and the table. Its contents appeared to be a dense fluid, white and pale azure, like to the gathering of a summer cloud, and incessantly rolling and mingling within the cylinder.

This lasted two minutes, when it began slowly to move before my sister-in-law; then following the oblong shape of the table, before my son and myself. Passing *behind* my wife, it paused for a moment over her right shoulder. (Observe, there was no mirror opposite to her in which she could then behold it.)

Instantly she crouched down and with both hands covering her shoulder, she shrieked out: 'Oh Christ! It has seized me!'

Even now while writing, I feel the fresh horror of that moment. I caught up my chair, struck at the wainscot behind her, then rushed upstairs to the other children's room and told the terrified nurse what I had seen.

Meanwhile, the other domestics had hurried to the parlour, where their mistress recounted to them the scene, even as I was detailing it upstairs. The marvel, or as some will say the absurdity of all this, is enhanced by the fact that neither my sister-in-law nor my son beheld the apparition, though to their mortal vision it was as apparent as to my wife's and mine.

Another strange manifestation was what a Guards officer described as 'a most queer and utterly distasteful atmosphere' as he approached the Bloody Tower one night. This 'atmosphere' filled him with such horror that for a moment his mind went blank, and the next thing he knew he was at the door of his mess nearly three hundred metres away. He had no recollection of fleeing from a sense of dread, but as he was training to take part in the Olympic Games at the time, his dash away from the scene must have been spectacular.

## Chapter 2

# Beware of Lady Margaret

If you should visit the beautiful ruins of Berry Pomeroy Castle in Devon, beware if you see a lady in old-fashioned clothing beckoning to you from the ramparts — legend tells that those who have followed her have fallen to their deaths! But Lady Margaret is only one of several ghosts which inhabit one of the most haunted castles in the south of England.

At first sight there is nothing to suggest the terrible things which have taken place there. Berry Pomeroy stands alone in the middle of beautiful hushed woodlands, a romantic ruin complete with massive towers and walls which surround the shell of what was once a magnificent house. In the late afternoon when the shadows lengthen and the rows of empty windows stare sightlessly at the setting sun do not be surprised if you shiver, for it is then that you can sense something very uncanny about the place.

The history of the castle goes back to the Norman Conquest when it was built by Ralph de la Pomerai who was one of the adventurers who crossed the Channel with Duke William, though the building we see today probably dates from the late thirteenth century and after. During the reign of Richard the Lion-Heart, Henry de la Pomerai sided with Prince John in his intrigues against his brother while he was away at the

Crusades. When Richard returned from the Holy Land he had grave doubts about Henry's loyalty and sent a herald to Berry Pomeroy to report on his real allegiance. When the herald had gathered the evidence, he challenged Henry to appear before the High Court on a treason charge.

Henry answered this with a dagger, killing the herald and fleeing to another of his castles at Tregony in Cornwall. Then, with a band of his henchmen, he took over the castle at St Michael's Mount where he was besieged by forces under the command of the Archbishop of Canterbury and the Sheriff of Cornwall. When he realised he could no longer hold out against them he committed suicide in the Roman fashion by having his veins opened by a surgeon. Because he had not been tried or condemned, King Richard allowed Berry Pomeroy Castle and its lands to remain the property of the Pomeroy family.

The Pomeroy ownership of the castle ended in 1549, a troubled year for England when Kett's rebellion broke out in Norfolk and another flared in the west of England in which Sir Thomas Pomeroy marched on Exeter with two thousand followers. He never took the city, being put to flight by an army under Lord Russell.

It was obvious castles could be strongholds for the rebels and royal orders came that some should be given up or demolished. According to legend, two brothers held the castle after the defeat of Sir Thomas and, having enjoyed independence and power, refused to bow to the command of the distant boy king, Edward VI – or rather that of his Protector, Edward Seymour, Earl of Hertford and Duke of Somerset.

The two knights hid their family treasure in the castle, buckled themselves in full armour and, having blindfolded their chargers, thundered out of the castle and galloped to the edge of the nearby cliff, where they hurtled into space, to die as free men in the valley below.

A great many years later this legend had a curious

aftermath. Two Totnes labourers, who were friends, each dreamed of a crock of gold hidden in one of the huge fireplaces in the ruined castle. For three nights running both men had the same dream, and on the fourth day they told each other about it. Struck by the significant fact that they had dreamed an identical dream, they decided to search for the treasure.

After their day's work was over they set off towards the castle, but as dusk fell a thunderstorm blew up and lightning flashed over the ruins. When they approached the wood surrounding the castle they met a local squire who warned them not to go near the ruins on such a night as it would be dangerous. The castle had already been struck by lightning and much of it had been destroyed in the fire which followed. Who could say that lightning might not strike again and dislodge more masonry?

When the two men told the squire of their dreams his insistence that they should not risk their lives was redoubled, and they returned to Totnes, deciding to come on the following day when the storm would be over.

The next evening they returned and found the crock in the fireplace just as it had been in their dream. The only difference was that it was empty. But by a strange coincidence the squire who had been so concerned for their safety seemed suddenly to have acquired great wealth.

The least sinister of the castle's ghosts are a pair of lovers who have been glimpsed on top of the gatehouse which is built between two great towers. Facing each other they try to hold hands, but the phantom fingers of each pass through the other's. There are two legends told to explain their plight, the first being rather like that of Romeo and Juliet in that they were the victims of a family feud. The daughter of the lord of the castle fell in love with a youth whose family had a long-standing and very bitter quarrel with the Pomeroys. Their forbidden romance came to a tragic end when the girl's father found them having a secret meeting in a rose garden and

18

ran his sword through the young man for the sake of family honour.

The other story describes how a certain Lord Berry was walking outside the walls of the castle with his beautiful cousin Genevieve when they were attacked by outlaws and knocked unconscious. When the girl opened her eyes again she found that she was in a cave with the dead bodies of her captors scattered around her. Leaning against the cave wall was Raby Copeland, Lord Berry's standard-bearer. Using bandages torn from her scarf to bind his wounds, she heard him explain how he had trailed the robbers to their cave where he had burst upon them in a rescue attempt. When she asked why he had risked his life to save her, he admitted that even though he knew his master wanted to marry her, he was in love with her himself. At this Genevieve confessed that she had been secretly in love with him and that she would never marry her cousin.

When retainers from the castle carried Raby Copeland back to Berry Pomeroy and put him in the gatehouse chamber, Genevieve told Lord Berry that she intended to marry his standard-bearer. In a jealous frenzy the lord of the castle struck the girl down and then went and slew her wounded lover.

Equally cruel and tragic is the castle's most famous ghost story which concerns two sisters, Eleanor and Margaret Pomeroy, who were both in love with the same man. Lady Eleanor, the elder of the two, was so jealous of Margaret that she used her powers as mistress of the castle to keep her locked in a dungeon beneath one of the towers (now known as St Margaret's Tower). The prisoner was allowed so little food that she was a living skeleton before she died in her dark and lonely vault. No doubt the evil Eleanor gloated over the way Margaret's once beautiful features had withered. No doubt she saw her way clear to the heart of the man she desired, but her crime was not to remain a secret — the tormented ghost of her sister from time to time returns from the dead as a reminder of the murder.

According to a booklet on the castle's legends by S. M. Ellis: 'Now on certain nights of the year, the lovely Margaret is said to arise from her entombed dungeon, leaving St Margaret's Tower, and walk along the ramparts in long flowing robes and beckon the beholder to come and join her in the dungeon below.'

Certainly this makes a very satisfying story for visitors to the picturesque ruins, but those who know the castle will tell you that there is something very strange about it, as though traces of ancient evil linger on.

Late one summer evening I arrived at Berry Pomeroy to photograph its ruins. It was past closing time but the lady who acts as caretaker said that she would take me to them as each evening she strolled through the woods to exercise her Alsatian dog.

When we arrived at the castle, she said, 'I shall show you something very strange.' She led me to one of two deep pits lined with masonry, and descended into it by means of worn steps. She then called to the dog to join her, and obediently the frisky young animal bounded in the direction of her voice. He leapt down the steps into the dungeon, threshing his tail in delight at having found his mistress in this game of hide-and-seek.

The lady came out and then stepped down into the second dungeon.

'This is the one in which Lady Margaret was imprisoned,' she explained, and again she called the Alsatian. Once again he bounded towards her, but a few feet away from the edge of the pit he halted as though he had a sheet of glass blocking his pathway. He crouched, belly flat, and whimpered softly.

'Good boy, good boy,' called his mistress. 'Come to me.'

Hearing her voice the dog took courage and seemed about to follow out her command. He jumped forward, but once again came to an abrupt halt, uttering a desolate wail. He was obviously torn by what he felt was his duty to obey his mistress and the unseen terror holding

20

him back. The lady, not wishing to be cruel, came out of the dungeon and told the dog to have a run. I could feel the relief with which he raced away into the woods.

'You see, to us there seems to be no difference between the two dungeons,' she said. 'But there is something *wrong* with that one.'

Another frightening ghost at Berry Pomeroy is the Blue Lady who, wearing a blue hooded cape, searches the grounds for her lost baby — which, according to legend, she smothered herself. What was alarming about her was that she was a harbinger of death in the days when the castle was inhabited.

One of the best descriptions of her comes down to us from a highly reliable source, Sir Walter Farquhar, whose lifetime dedication to medicine was rewarded with a baronetcy in 1796. A short time before the doctor gained his title he had been residing in Torquay and a professional call had taken him to Berry Pomeroy.

When the wheels of his carriage crunched to a halt by Seymour Lodge — now only a great façade with staring windows — he was shown into a dark but handsomely furnished room. Rays of light filtered through diamond-shaped frames of stained glass, splashing a pattern of luminous colours on to a black staircase which led to apartments above.

Minutes passed and just as the doctor began to get impatient a door opened and a young woman entered dressed in a richly embroidered gown. Thinking she was a member of the household come to escort him to the sickroom, the doctor took a step forward, but he was completely ignored by the silent girl. Nervously twisting her hands together, she crossed to the foot of the stairs, hesitated a moment and then ascended until the light from the window caught her features like a multi-coloured spotlight.

Sir Walter afterwards wrote: 'If ever human face exhibited agony and remorse; if ever eye, that index of the soul, portrayed anguish uncheered by hope, and

21

suffering without interval; if ever features betrayed that within the wearer's bosom there dwelt a hell, those features and that being were then presented to me.'

Just after the silent figure appeared to quit the room, the caretaker of the castle walked in, doubtless apologising for the delay, and took the doctor to his wife, whose illness was so severe that Sir Walter temporarily forgot the strange figure which had ignored him. When he returned to Berry Pomeroy the next morning he found his patient had rallied, and once out of her bedroom he asked the caretaker about the mysterious young woman he had seen the previous afternoon.

According to Sir Walter, the caretaker exclaimed: 'My poor wife! My poor wife! That it should come to this. You don't know the strange, awful story – and his lordship is extremely against any allusion ever being made to the tale or any importance being attached to it – but I must and will tell you! You have seen the ghost of the daughter of a former baron of Berry Pomeroy. Now, whenever death is about to come to anybody in the castle, the crazed phantom is seen. . . . When my son was drowned she was seen – now it is my wife.'

'But your wife is better,' argued Sir Walter. 'All immediate danger is over.'

The caretaker replied that for thirty years he had lived in the castle and he had never known the omen go unfulfilled. This annoyed the doctor and he said, 'It is absurd to talk about omens. I trust to see your wife recovered.'

But several hours later she was dead!

Soon afterwards, when he had been appointed physician to the Prince of Wales who later became George IV, Sir Walter was one of the most sought-after doctors in England. One day a lady came to his consulting room to ask his advice about her sister whom she described as 'sinking' through depression following the shock of a supernatural experience. She explained that one morning they had driven from Torquay to Berry

Pomeroy to see the romantic ruins with their brother. When they arrived they learned that the caretaker was dangerously ill, in fact he died during their visit.

Not wishing to cause any disturbance at such a time, the lady and her brother went to find the keys for themselves, leaving their sister in a large room in the lodge with a dark staircase in it.

Having found the keys they returned to find her muttering wildly about a phantom figure.

'I know that you will say all this is quite preposterous,' the lady said to Sir Walter. 'Indeed, we have tried to treat the matter with scorn and to laugh my sister out of it. But when we joke, she only grows more agitated.'

'I must tell you, before I attend to your sister, that this is no delusion,' said Sir Walter. 'I myself have seen the same figure in somewhat similar circumstances. Believe me, it is no joking matter.'

The next day he visited the lady and, with his special understanding of her case, it was not long before she recovered from her illness. It was not for her the Blue Lady had appeared, but for the caretaker!

A more cheerful tradition connected with Berry Pomeroy refers to a tree — believed to be over a century old — which grows close to the castle wall and is known as the Wishing Tree. All you have to do is walk round it backwards three times, being careful not to trip over its great roots, and your wish will be fulfilled.

*Chapter 3*

# Windsor's Wild Huntsman

Windsor Castle's most spectacular ghost is Herne the Hunter, who over the centuries has been seen leading the Wild Hunt in the Great Park. To have seen this glowing figure must have been a terrifying experience because he has been described as having antlers growing from his head.

The story of Herne goes back to the reign of Richard II, when he was a keeper in the royal forest. One day as the king was hunting a wounded stag rounded on him and would have gored him had not Herne leapt on the animal and plunged his knife into it. But as he did so the animal caught Herne with its antlers, and when the huntsman was dragged clear it was obvious that he was dying.

At that moment a mysterious stranger walked out of the trees and told the king that if he agreed to his magical treatment he could save Herne's life. Richard gave his assent and the man removed the stag's antlers and bandaged them to Herne's head. He then asked that Herne be taken on a litter to his hut where he would nurse him until he was healed.

As he was carried away the grateful king told Herne that when he was well again he would be appointed head huntsman. This made the rest of the hunters jealous and by the time they reached the forest hut they were determined that their order of promotion should not be upset by Herne. They told the wizard that if he wanted to save his own life he must make sure that Herne did not recover.

The old man replied that as Herne was under his protection he could not physically harm him, but if they dared to risk Herne's curse he would see to it that he did not remain hunt leader for long. The men may have scoffed at the idea of a curse, but only for a short while — when Herne returned as leader he was suffering from loss of memory as far as the Great Park was concerned. It was as though he had forgotten the geography of the forest and the tracks along which the deer ran, and each hunt he led was a failure. After many disappointing days of sport, the king lost his temper and dismissed him.

Embittered by the disgrace, Herne committed suicide the same night, hanging himself from the branch of a huge oak tree which until 1863 — when it was blown down during a gale — was known as Herne's Oak.

One of the hunters who had forced the wizard to bring about Herne's downfall was walking through a grove when he saw the body swinging in the wind. He raced to tell his companions but when they returned there was no trace of the body, but from then on the misfortune which had befallen Herne befell them. Soon the king was so annoyed with their ineptitude that they realised they too were in danger of dismissal. Fearfully they went to the forest wizard, who explained that until they had made atonement to the earthbound spirit of Herne they would have no luck.

Following his instruction they congregated about the old tree after dark. At midnight the phantom of Herne, complete with antlers, appeared and, leaping on to a ghostly horse, commanded them to follow him through the forest. For the rest of the night the wild hunt combed the forest for deer and was so successful that when King Richard went hunting there was not an animal left for him to chase.

Realising there was something uncanny going on, he

25

forced the truth from one of the hunters. That night he went to Herne's Oak where the phantom huntsman appeared at midnight. He promised Richard that if those who had betrayed him were punished, he would cease to haunt the wood as long as he reigned. The king agreed and next morning ordered the conspirators to be hanged, after which he had no more trouble in finding game in Windsor Park.

After the king was murdered by his enemies in 1400, the ghost of Herne the Hunter was seen again in the Great Park. His last reported appearance was shortly before the Second World War, and a story circulated that whenever England was faced with troubled times the ghost of the hunter would appear.

After Herne's Oak had been blown down, Queen Victoria ordered that a new one should be planted in its place to keep the tradition alive.

Not surprisingly, Windsor Castle is haunted by royal ghosts. The oldest of these is Henry VIII who can be heard moving painfully along a certain corridor. As a young man he was a splendid sportsman, but as he grew older he became fat and a ghastly ulcer in his leg caused him to limp. It is the sound of his weary, shuffling walk that has survived down the centuries, coupled with the sound of wheezing breath.

Much more elegant is the spectre of Elizabeth I. In February 1897 Carr Glynn, a lieutenant in the Grenadier Guards, was reading in one of the rooms of the Queen's Library when he saw a lady, dressed in black and wearing a lace scarf of the same colour over her hair and shoulders, walk out of an inner room and cross the chamber. He heard the sound of her shoes on the polished wood floor and could almost have touched her as she walked past him, crossed the room and disappeared into a corner.

At first Lieutenant Glynn thought she must have gone through a doorway into another room. A moment later one of the castle servants entered the reading room and the lieutenant questioned him as to the identity of the dark lady. The man replied that nobody had entered the room.

Greatly mystified, Lieutenant Glynn rose and went to the room into which he had seen the lady disappear. It was empty and there was no exit by which she could have left!

The attendant then told him hesitantly that he must have glimpsed the ghost of Queen Elizabeth. She had been seen before, walking across the library in exactly the same way as the Guards officer described.

Charles I is said to revisit the Canon's House which stands in the castle's grounds. Although many ghosts of those prisoners who knelt before the executioner appear headless, the shade of the tragic king is complete, the face having the same sad expression as shown in his famous portraits.

The reign of George III was marred by the monarch's bouts of madness, though this did nothing to diminish the love his subjects felt for him. They nicknamed him 'Farmer George' because of his intense interest in horticulture, and his popularity was proved by the universal delight — and the monuments — which celebrated his return to sanity. But for the last nine years of his life, from 1811 when the Prince of Wales was appointed regent, the king was in a state of permanent mental derangement, passing his days in a room at Windsor playing on his harp. Now his spectre returns to the apartments where he was restrained.

Apart from royal ghosts, the most illustrious spirit to have appeared in Windsor Castle is that of Sir George Villiers, the father of the ambitious Duke of Buckingham who, as the favourite of James I, became the most influential man in the kingdom. After the death of James, Buckingham retained his position of power through his friendship with the new king, Charles I, and became one of the most disliked men in England.

Edward Hyde, the first Earl of Clarendon, wrote in 1707 that Buckingham was so unpopular that prophecies of his death became widespread. No doubt these were merely forms of wishful thinking but Clarendon wrote: 'Among the rest there was one which was upon a better foundation of credit than usually such stories are founded upon. In February 1628, an officer at Windsor Castle woke one night to see a man of very venerable aspect, who drew the curtains of his bed, and, fixing his eyes upon him, asked if he knew him.'

The startled officer did not reply at first, but at length managed to mutter that the midnight visitor resembled Sir George Villiers.

The ghost replied that he was right, and said that he wanted him to perform an errand. He should go to his son the Duke of Buckingham and warn him that 'if he did not somewhat to ingratiate himself to the people, or at least to abate the extreme malice they had against him, he would be suffered to live but a short time.'

Then the phantom faded away and the officer, thinking he had been the victim of a nightmare, drifted back into sleep.

The next night the ghost reappeared, and again asked the officer to go to his son with the message. Still the officer ignored the request, believing in the morning light that it was nothing but a recurring dream.

On the third night Sir George manifested yet again, begging him to warn the duke. The officer, now accustomed to these visitations, answered that it would be difficult to get the duke to take notice of such a wild tale, whereupon the ghost confided in him 'two or three particulars' which he said he must not mention to anybody but the duke.

Convinced at last that he had seen a real ghost, the officer rode to London the next day and managed to get himself admitted into the Buckingham household.

Afterwards the officer said that when he mentioned 'those particulars which were to gain him credit',

Buckingham went white. Having listened to the warning, the duke went hunting with Charles I, but it was obvious to the rest of the party that his heart was not in it and very soon he left the field. He rode to his mother's house where he stayed with her for three hours, talking so excitedly that the sound of their voices came through the wall of the room where they were closeted.

Clarendon wrote that when Buckingham left his mother 'his countenance appeared full of trouble, with a mixture of anger, a countenance that was never before observed in him in any conversation with her, towards whom he had a profound reverence.'

On 23 August of that year the Duke of Buckingham was assassinated at Portsmouth by a discontented subaltern named John Felton who overnight became a popular hero.

Clarendon concluded: 'Whatever there was of all this it is a notorious truth that when the news of the Duke's murder was made known to his mother, she seemed not in the least surprised, but received it as if she had foreseen it. . . .'

Windsor Castle's other ghosts include that of a Grenadier guardsman who committed suicide while on sentry duty and whose phantom is still sometimes glimpsed in the moonlight in the Long Walk of the Great Park, and the spectre of William of Wykeham who designed parts of the castle in the fourteenth century. At night he has been seen on the Round Tower, looking upon his six-centuries-old work with an expression of satisfaction.

29

*Chapter 4*

# Unholy Hermitage

If ever a castle looks as though it has a story that will freeze your blood it is Hermitage, a huge square fortress which looms high in the heart of the lonely moors south of Hawick. It is surrounded by earthworks which are probably much older than the building itself, and which make it look as though the ground is swallowing up its foundations. Sir Walter Scott, who claimed it was his favourite castle, wrote: 'The Castle of Hermitage unable to support the load of iniquity which had been long accumulating within its walls, is supposed to have partly sunk beneath the ground; and its ruins are still regarded by the peasants with peculiar aversion and horror.'

What was it about this great ruin which could arouse such aversion and horror? Certainly it had more than its share of dark deeds committed within its massive walls, and even the official guidebook admits 'it has had a colourful history, highly charged with cruel and mournful memories'.

It was built in the thirteenth century to guard the western approach to Scotland, and a century later the Scottish chronicler John of Fordoun wrote that in 1242 England and Scotland nearly came to war because the Scots had erected in Liddesdale 'a certain castle which is called Hermitage'.

Another early account states that in the year 1300

Edward I ordered it to be repaired at a cost of £20, and in the century which followed the possession of the castle frequently changed hands between the Scots and English. In 1338 it became the property of Sir William Douglas, the famous Knight of Liddesdale, after which followed a period of confusion and slaughter.

Four years after taking the castle Sir William starved a prisoner, Sir Alexander Ramsay, to death. When he later changed sides and threw his lot in with the English, David II of Scotland gave Hermitage to another William, later the first Earl of Douglas. He guaranteed his right to the property by murdering Sir William Douglas in Ettrick Forest. Sir William's widow then married a member of the Dacre family who, with the might of Edward III behind him, took the castle back into English hands.

Later it belonged to the fourth Earl of Bothwell who blew up with gunpowder the house in which Lord Darnley, the husband of Mary Queen of Scots, was sleeping so that he could marry Mary himself.

With such a tradition of treachery and bloodshed it is only to be expected that the gaunt shell is haunted, but the ghost of Hermitage goes back further than the terrible death of Sir Alexander Ramsay, to one of the first owners, Lord William Soulis, who in the thirteenth century was the hereditary King's Butler of Scotland. According to legend his phantom returns once every seven years to Hermitage where, in an underground chamber, he keeps a tryst with an evil spirit. Lord Soulis, whose wickedness eclipsed that of any of the lords who followed him, had an arch enemy in the huge Cout of Keilder — the name Cout was a local word meaning 'colt' so that the nickname suggested someone fast and strong.

One day the Cout rode to Hermitage and reining up his warhorse before the gateway, shouted a challenge to Lord Soulis to meet him in combat. He must have felt very confident as he did so because tradition says that he was clad in magical armour which made it impossible for him to be wounded.

He did not have to wait long under the frowning walls of the castle before the gate opened and out thundered Lord Soulis in shining armour which unluckily for him had been forged without magic spells. The two Border lords hurtled towards each other with their lances lowered. Lord Soulis deflected the steel tip of his enemy's weapon with his shield, but though his own lance struck the Cout's helmet the wooden shaft shattered and the impact threw both men to the ground.

After they had struggled upright, the combatants continued their duel on foot. One can imagine the echoes ringing as broadsword clashed against broadsword and the breath of the warriors wheezed within their helmets, but although Lord Soulis was a more skilful fighter his sweeping blows seemed to have no effect on his enemy. And as he felt his sword vibrate strangely in his hand each time it struck the Cout's armour, he began to understand that he was facing uncanny powers.

Lord Soulis had no objection to ignoring the rules of chivalry, and he called to his retainers to come to his aid. When the Cout saw a determined band of spearmen emerge from the castle, he turned and fled towards Hermitage Water, a small river to which was joined the castle's moat. Here his pursuers flung him down the bank, and now aware that conventional weapons could not harm him, held his head beneath the surface until the bubbles ceased to issue from his magic helmet.

Close to the ruin of Hermitage Chapel (built in 1170 by a hermit known as Brother William who thus gave the castle its name) you can still see a mound marked out with stones which is believed to be the grave of the drowned Cout. The foundations of this chapel are less than two hundred metres along Hermitage Water from the castle.

After seeing the effectiveness of enchanted armour, Lord Soulis decided to become a magician himself, and in his experiments he 'raised' a demon known as Robin Redcap — his cap being dyed that colour with blood.

32

And it was blood that this terrifying imp desired, promising that in return for human sacrifices he would grant the Border lord the supernatural powers he wanted, though he imposed one strange condition — Lord Soulis should never look at him. All he knew of Robin Redcap was the voice of the evil spirit coming from behind him.

In order to pay Robin his terrible tribute, Lord Soulis used the blood of kidnapped children in black magic rituals which took place in an underground dungeon which is still to be seen. One of the benefits the demon bestowed on the sorcerer was the promise that he could never be hurt by iron or hemp, making him safe from hanging or injury by steel weapons.

An old Border ballad ran:

Lord Soulis he sat in Hermitage Castle,
　And beside him Old Redcap sly —
'Now, tell me, thou sprite, who are mickle of might,
　The death that I must die.'

The demon replied that Lord Soulis would not die:

'Till threefold ropes of sifted sand
　Around thy body twine.'

Thinking himself to be invincible, the cruel lord of Hermitage committed outrage after outrage without fear of retribution. He could call up Robin Redcap whenever he wished by tapping three times on an iron chest, but on one occasion he was either curious or careless and he saw Redcap, with the result that the spirit had the right to claim his soul. He, however, kept to the agreement and, as long as Lord Soulis remained alive, he protected him as he had promised.

He continued to terrorise the district until the local people could take no more. Rumours of the fate of the unusually large number of missing children began to circulate, so they sought the advice of the wizard Thomas of Ercildoune who told them how they could dispose of the tyrant without Robin Redcap being able to save him.

The furious parents of the missing children of Liddesdale revolted against their overlord and managed to capture him outside Hermitage Castle. Knowing that their ropes and billhooks could not harm him, they rolled him up in a sheet of lead and carried him to a spot known as Nine Stane Rig. Then, according to the ballad:

On a circle of stones they placed the pot,
　On a circle of stones but barely nine;
They heated it red and fiery hot,
　And the burnished brass did glimmer and shine.
They rolled him up in a sheet of lead –
　A sheet of lead for a funeral pall;
They plunged him into the cauldron red,
　And melted him body, lead, bones, and all.

Although the wicked lord was melted down, his spirit still has to rendezvous with Robin Redcap every seven years in the same underground chamber where once he performed his bloody rites. Legend tells that he gave the castle key to the spirit and with it the secret of his ill-gotten treasure.

Today the atmosphere surrounding Hermitage Castle can be very creepy, this description by the famous journalist W. T. Stead being a typical example of what some people feel there:

'I unlocked the door with the key, which I had brought with me from the keeper's cottage, at a little distance down the valley. As it creaked on its hinges and I felt the chill air of the ruin, I was almost afraid to enter. Mustering my courage, however, I went in and explored the castle, then lying down on the mossy bank I gave myself up to the glamour of the past. I must have been there an hour or more when suddenly, while the blood seemed to freeze down my back, I was startled by a loud prolonged screech, over my head, followed by a noise which I could only compare to the trampling of a multitude of iron-shod feet through the stone paved doorway. This was alarming enough, but it was nothing to the horror which filled me when I heard the heavy gate swing on its hinges with a clang which for the moment seemed like the closing of a vault in which I was entombed alive. I could almost hear the beating of my heart. . . . When I had recovered from my fright, I ventured into the echoing doorway to see whether or not I was really a prisoner. The door was shut, and I remember to this day the tremor which I experienced when I laid my hand upon the door and tried whether or not it was locked. It yielded to my hand, and I have seldom felt a sense of more profound relief than when I stepped across the threshold and felt that I was free once more. . . .

Another castle which has a frightening legend connected with blood-letting is Alnwick in Northumberland. In this case the villain was not a sorcerer but a vampire which terrorised those living in the shadow of the castle's ramparts.

Today the castle is a splendid place to visit — it has been described as 'the Windsor Castle of the North' — and one of its unusual features is the statues of warriors on its walls which were put there in the old days to fool an approaching enemy.

Gilbert de Tesson, who had been William the Conqueror's standard-bearer at the Battle of Hastings, was the first Norman master of Alnwick. After he rebelled against William Rufus, the site passed to Yvo de Vesci who began to build a fortification there as a protection against Scottish raiders. The present castle was begun by his son-in-law, Eustace Fitzjohn, in 1140. It was attacked on several occasions by the Scots, in 1405 it fell to Henry IV when its then owner, Henry Percy, rebelled against him, and it was besieged in 1462 during the Wars of the Roses.

In his *Historia Rerum Anglicarum*, William of Newburgh, the chronicler who lived in the twelfth

35

century, described how a deceased master of the castle — 'a stranger to God's race and whose crimes were many' — would rise from his tomb during the hours of darkness to prowl the streets of the sleeping town.

The local priest told the historian how his body left such a stench of death and corruption behind him that pestilence broke out and may citizens fled from Alnwick in fear of the bloodthirsting monster. A group of men, blaming the vampire for the plague, banded together to rid themselves of the menace.

William wrote: 'They armed themselves, therefore, with sharp spades and betaking themselves to the cemetery, they began to dig. And whilst they yet thought they would have to dig much deeper, suddenly they came upon the body covered with but a thin layer of earth. It was gorged and swollen with a frightful corpulence. . . .'

One of the men struck the bloated body with the edge of his spade and from the wound came a gush of fresh blood, proving that it was indeed a vampire. Immediately the corpse was taken beyond the precincts of Alnwick and burned to ashes. After this the pestilence subsided.

This story is unusual in that it is about a vampire. I know of only one other account of such a creature in England, and this shows that our ghosts are not quite as nasty as those in European countries, which can produce hundreds of vampire tales.

## Chapter 5

# The Horrors of Glamis

Glamis Castle is famous as the childhood home of the Queen Mother, whose ancestors have held it for six centuries — but it is also one of the world's most haunted castles. It has long had an eerie reputation, as this description published a century ago proves. It was written by the Reverend F. G. Lee, an author who studied the supernatural.

There is no doubt about the reality of the noises at Glamis Castle. On one occasion, some years ago, the head of the family, with several companions, was determined to investigate the cause. One night, when the disturbance was greater and more violent than usual, and it should be premised strange, weird and unearthly sounds had often been heard, and by many persons, some quite unacquainted with the ill repute of the Castle, his lordship went to the Haunted Room, opened the door with a key, and dropped back in a dead swoon into the arms of his companions; nor could he ever be induced to open his lips on the subject afterwards.

But before we investigate the sealed room, let us take a look at the castle. When the summer sun warms its reddish walls and turrets with candle-snuffer roofs, and throws shadows on its sundial with over eighty faces, it is like an illustration from a fairy tale. But in the winter, when its spires seem to pierce the low-flying clouds or the mist eddies round its battlements, it could be a film setting for Count Dracula.

We know little of the castle's early history apart from the Shakespearean tradition that Macbeth, the Thane of Glamis, stabbed Duncan to death in a gloomy chamber still known as Duncan's Hall. Six years earlier, in 1034, Glamis had been the scene of Malcolm II's assassination, and for many generations the stain of his royal blood could not be removed from the floor.

Records begin in 1372 when King Robert II gave it to his son-in-law Sir John Lyon. When he came to Glamis he brought with him an heirloom in the form of a cup, and it was the removal of this talisman from its original home which was thought to be responsible for the sinister things which happened after it arrived at the castle.

The climax of the family's misfortunes came in 1537 when Janet Douglas, widow of the sixth Lord of Glamis, was arrested for practising witchcraft. William Lyon accused her of using black magic in an attempt to kill James V of Scotland, also accusing her son and her second husband Archibald Campbell, who fell to a merciful death while attempting to escape from Edinburgh Castle.

Lady Janet's death was far more terrible. Tied to a stake on Castle Hill she was burned alive as a witch, though she met her fate — according to an old chronicle — 'with great commiseration of the people, being in the prime of the years, of a singular beauty, and suffering all, though a woman, with a manlike courage'. It is her ghost which has been seen surrounded by a fiery glow floating above the clock tower of Glamis Castle.

Her son survived for, although he too had been sentenced to death, the court ruled that the execution must wait until he reached his twenty-first birthday — by which time William Lyon, who had laid the charge against the family, had made a deathbed confession that he made up the story out of spite. The young man was released and his estates were restored to him.

One of the eerie manifestations which from time to time take place at Glamis is an inexplicable knocking which some believe is a ghostly echo from the building of the scaffold on which Lady Janet was put to death.

A different explanation for the sounds goes back to the time of a bitter feud between the Ogilvies and Lindsays. After a clan battle, a party of defeated Ogilvies straggled into Glamis in search of protection. The lord of the castle had no wish to arouse the anger of the fugitives by refusing them sanctuary, on the other hand he was afraid of the wrath of the Lindsays by giving it. He therefore conducted the Ogilvies to a remote room where he promised them they would be safe. Once the unsuspecting clansmen were inside he slammed the heavy door, turned the key and left them hammering on it in despair.

One story tells that their remains were not found until Victorian times when Lord Strathmore forced open the ancient door and fainted at the sight which met his gaze. It was suggested that he beheld a mound of skeletons, some of which still had the bones of their arms clamped between their teeth as they had tried to keep death at bay by eating their own flesh.

Sir Walter Scott, writing about Glamis, said, 'It contains also a curious monument of the peril of feudal times, being a secret chamber, the entrance of which, by the law or custom of the family, must only be known to three persons at once, viz. the Earl of Strathmore, his heir apparent, and any third person whom they may take into their confidence.'

The legend of a secret room in the castle is well known — it is what inhabits it which is the puzzle. Of the many theories advanced, the most popular is that a grotesquely deformed child — the result of a curse laid on the family — was imprisoned in it. A typical version of this story appeared in the *Daily Telegraph* of 28 October 1966:

The walls in the old castle are immensely thick — up to 15 feet in places. Somewhere in them lies the secret of Glamis — a mysterious chamber where a previous Earl is supposed to have kept hidden a hideous monster, a son born half man, half beast.

For 150 years the monster lived in the castle, only emerging to crawl about at night. . . .

One historical fact adds support to the legend. A portrait in the drawing-room shows the 1st Earl with his sons: two boys and a peculiar little dwarf.

There is a rumour in circulation that the imprisoned monster died in 1921 — something with such a long life span would be supernatural rather than human.

Another story is that a long time ago a servant was found to be a blood-sucking vampire and was locked in the secret room where he has remained in a trance ever since, his ancient flesh uncorrupted and his dreadful thirst waiting to be quenched with the unsealing of his crypt.

A completely different explanation for the horror of the secret chamber goes back to Alexander, the terrible fourth Earl of Crawford, nicknamed in his day 'Earl Beardie'. In *The Picture of Scotland*, published in 1827, Robert Chambers wrote:

It is the tradition of Glamis that he [Earl Beardie] was playing at cards in the Castle, when, being warned to desist, as he was losing, he swore, in a transport of fury, that he would play till the day of judgement. On this the devil appeared in the company, and they, room and all, disappeared.

According to local folklore the forbidden room was the scene of a card game between the Devil and one of the lords of Glamis known by his retainers as Earl Patie. One stormy Sunday night in a November long ago, the earl paced restlessly up and down his hall. Because of the Scottish attitude to the Lord's Day, he had not been able to raise a hunting party and now he was dangerously bored. Suddenly he shouted for a deck of cards, and then looked about for partners. The ladies of Glamis were at evensong in the chapel, the servants remained out of sight, afraid their master would force them to profane the Sabbath. He even tried to bully a priest into taking a hand — and received a sermon in reply, so 'swearing tremendously' and declaring he would be happy to play with the Devil himself, he took the pack and retired to a chamber in the old tower.

As one expects from such old stories, it was not long before a knock shook the door and a deep voice demanded if the earl wanted a partner. The earl retorted that he did and a dark stranger, wrapped in a black cloak, limped in, seated himself at the table and picked up the cards. No doubt the earl felt a pang of unease as he looked at his mysterious guest — especially after his rash declaration — but the madness was upon him and soon he forgot his doubts in the excitement of the game.

Finally the stranger suggested a stake so high that the earl was forced to admit that he had not the gold to match it, but, he added, if he lost he would put his name to any bond the stranger might draw up.

He lost, and when he died five years later he must have discovered the nature of the hellish agreement he had signed. For a long time ghostly sounds — echoes from that satanic card game — tormented the castle inhabitants. Finally the room in which the evil lingered was locked and the passage leading to it sealed with a thick wall of masonry.

A widely reported story connected with the sealed chamber goes back to the 1880s when guests at a house party there planned to find it while their host was away in Edinburgh. As there are over a hundred rooms in the castle it was no easy task, but ingeniously they entered every possible room and hung towels from its windows. When they assembled outside there remained a single window from which no cloth hung, but before they were able to investigate further the earl returned unexpectedly and was furious at their behaviour.

Apart from the hidden room, Glamis Castle abounds in more conventional ghosts. A White Lady has been seen to glide along the avenue leading to the castle. Another spectre is a very tall, spindly figure known as 'Jack the Runner', while a little black servant — believed to have been the victim of ill-treatment — has materialised by the door of the sitting room used by the Queen Mother.

The Reverend Lee described a phantom warrior:

A lady and her child were staying for a few days at the Castle. The child was asleep in an adjoining dressing-room, and the lady, having gone to bed, lay awake for a while. Suddenly a cold blast stole into the room, extinguishing the night-light by her bedside, but not affecting the one in the dressing-room beyond, in which her child had its cot. By that light she saw a tall mailed figure pass into the dressing-room in which she was lying. Immediately thereafter there was a shriek from the child. Her maternal instinct was aroused. She rushed into the dressing-room and found the child in an agony of fear. It described what it had seen as a giant who had come and leant over its face.

An extraordinary dream coincidence about Glamis was related by Mrs Maglagan, the wife of a former Archbishop of York. As Lord Strathmore's sister-in-law she was a frequent visitor to the castle, but her dream actually took place at Tulliallan Castle on the night of 28 September, 1869. After going to bed she dreamed she was at Glamis watching some horses in the park when the dinner gong sounded. Afraid of being late, she hurried towards the Blue Room, where she slept on her visits, to change her clothes, but in the corridor she met a housemaid holding pieces of rusted iron.

'Where did you find those?' she asked the girl.

The maid told her that she had been cleaning the grate

in the Blue Room when she noticed a stone slab with a ring set in it. She had pulled at the ring and raised the stone, and in a hollow beneath it she had found the iron fragments.

'I'll take them down with me,' Mrs Maglagan said. 'His lordship likes to see everything that is found in the castle.'

Then, in her own words, 'As I opened the door of the Blue Room the thought crossed my mind: "They say the ghost always appears if anything is found. I wonder if he will come to me." I went in and there, seated in an armchair by the fire, I saw a huge figure of a man with a very long beard and an enormous stomach, which rose and fell with his breathing. I shook all over with terror, but walked to the fireplace and sat down on the coalbox staring at the ghost. Although he was breathing heavily I saw clearly that it was the face of a dead man.'

Still in her dream, Mrs Maglagan found the silence unendurable. To break the tension she held up the pieces of iron, saying, 'Look what I have found.'

The phantom sighed.

'Yes, you have lifted a great weight off me,' he said. 'Those irons have been weighing me down ever since. . . .'

'Ever since when?' asked the archbishop's wife.

'Ever since 1486.'

'At that moment, to my great relief, I heard a knock at the door,' Mrs Maglagan wrote. It was her maid, who opened the shutters to let the sun stream cheerfully into the room. 'I sat up in bed and found that my nightgown was quite wet with perspiration. I came downstairs very full of my dream, and still more of the fact, as I believed, that although the room was in all other respects exactly like the one I thought I remembered so well, the fireplace was in a different corner. So persuaded was I of that that next year I saw the room at Glamis and found that my dream memory was right and my waking memory wrong, I could scarcely believe my eyes.'

Two years later a Mrs Wingfield met Mrs Maglagan's

brother Eric and, having heard about his sister's curious dream, told him of an extraordinary coincidence. While Mrs Maglagan had been staying at Tulliallan, Mrs Wingfield had been a guest at Glamis, and on the same night Mrs Maglagan had had her dream, she had dreamed too.

She was occupying the Blue Room and went to bed as usual. After dozing off she suddenly awoke with the sensation that she was not alone in the room. She sat up and saw, seated before the fire, a 'huge old man with a long flowing beard'. He turned and gazed at her and she realised that, although he appeared to be breathing, 'the face was that of a dead man. . . .'

A frightening episode was witnessed by another guest at Glamis one night when he was looking out of his window into the castle quadrangle and became aware of the white face of a girl with an agonised expression gazing in silent appeal from a barred window opposite his. It was a minute before the great clock, whose heavy tick has been likened to the heartbeat of the castle, was to strike midnight. Suddenly the face vanished, as though dragged away by some unseen gaoler, and a despairing scream echoed across the courtyard.

The bewildered guest remained gazing at the empty window until he saw an ugly old woman emerge from a doorway at the base of a tower, carrying what appeared to be a large bundle or sack in her arms. Seeing the guest looking down at her, the hag hoisted the bundle over her shoulder and made off at good speed, leaving the guest with the uncanny feeling that the sacking contained the girl whose frightened face he had seen at the window.

There is an odd sequel to the story. Some years later the guest was caught in a snowstorm in a mountainous region of Italy and sought shelter at a monastery. During his stay there the monks told him a curious story of a woman who lived in a nearby convent. Her tongue had been cut out and her hands amputated at the wrists. The monks said that they believed she had been mutilated in this way to prevent her revealing some terrible family secret she had discovered – a large sum of money had been provided for her maintenance from an unknown source. The traveller was convinced that this mysterious person was none other than the girl he had briefly glimpsed at Glamis.

Unfortunately I have not been able to discover anything more about this story, not even when it was supposed to have happened, but one of the ghostly manifestations sometimes seen at the castle is the frightened face of a girl at a high window.

There is no shortage of other supernatural incidents connected with the castle, but let us look at just one more, which was described by the Victorian writer Augustus Hare. He was staying at the castle when one night a fellow guest looked out of his window to see a black coach drive up to the castle – without the normal scrunch of gravel – and pull up below him. A minute passed, then the driver looked up and, flicking the backs of his black horses with the reins, drove off in the direction from which he had come. The guest was impressed by his 'marked and terrible face'.

At breakfast the next morning he remarked to Lord Strathmore, 'You had a very late arrival last night.' At his account of the sinister coachman the earl went pale and answered in a low voice that no one had arrived at the castle.

Some weeks later the same man was staying in Paris on the third floor of a hotel. One day he rang for the lift, and when it arrived and the gates opened he jumped back in shocked surprise – the lift operator appeared identical to the mysterious coachman. Seeing the guest hesitate, the operator impatiently clashed the gates together. An instant later a cable snapped and the cage hurtled down the well. All its occupants were killed in the impact.

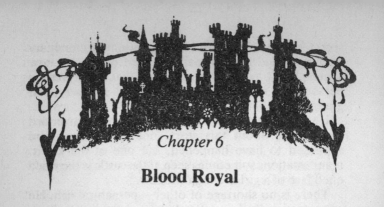

## Chapter 6

# Blood Royal

One of the earliest supernatural events connected with an English king took place a thousand years ago at Corfe Castle whose ruined keep rears above a quaint village of the same name in Dorset.

King Edward – known in history as Edward the Martyr – was fifteen years old when his father King Edgar died in 975. The late king had married twice and had a second son named Ethelred by his second wife Queen Elfrida. She had tried to get her own son crowned but her attempt failed and the elder son was proclaimed the rightful king. Hiding her anger, the queen retired to Corfe Castle with young Ethelred, who was later to be nicknamed 'The Unready'.

On 18 March 978 King Edward was hunting when he saw the distant bulk of the castle silhouetted against the cold sky and decided to pay his stepmother a courtesy call. He was probably more eager to see his half-brother Ethelred as there was a strong bond of affection between him and the ten-year-old boy. The hunting party had separated while chasing a deer, and the king was alone as he urged his horse in the direction of the castle.

A sentry recognised him as he approached and sent word to the queen so she could greet her royal stepson in the traditional manner. With Ethelred beside her, and flanked by her retainers, she waited as the solitary rider halted at the twin towers of the gate. (It is now known as the Martyr's Gate and as the walls of the castle were later expanded is no longer its main entrance.) The company bowed and several servants moved forward. One held the bridle of Edward's horse, another handed him the customary welcoming wine cup, while a third seized the king's free hand and made as though to kiss it. With the goblet in his sword hand, Edward was surprised at the sudden vicelike grip on his left hand.

'Why do you hold me so?' he asked with a laugh. He was to know the next instant as he felt a dagger thud into his unprotected back. He jerked his arm free and spurred his horse. The animal reared, Edward turned it round and, scattering the queen's henchmen, galloped away from the gate. But already he was reeling in the saddle, and halfway down the hill he fell from his mount. One foot was caught in the stirrup and the dying king was dragged to the bottom of the hill where the horse came to a halt by a brook.

With the mysterious disappearance of the king, Ethelred ascended the throne as Elfrida had planned. But now the supernatural comes into the story. Local people noticed that a mysterious ray of light shone from a well mouth near the castle. Word spread that it was a sign of some dark mystery and the well was searched. The body of the murdered king was brought to the surface, and on 18 February 979 it was buried at the church of St Mary of Wareham.

It was found that the well in which the body had been hidden had gained miraculous healing properties and it was named St Edward's Fountain. Meanwhile a local woman came forth with an amazing story. Before the assassins took the body to the well they hid it under a covering in her hut, confident that she could never witness against them as she was blind. At midnight the room was filled with a strange light – the woman knew because suddenly her sight was restored.

As a result of such manifestations Edward was declared a saint by the Pope.

Another cruel event in the history of the castle occurred when King John had twenty-two French prisoners starved to death in its dungeon.

A more inspiring episode took place during the Civil War when, in May 1643, the Parliamentary authorities sent a detachment of forty soldiers to the castle to requisition four small cannons they knew protected its massive walls. They did not expect trouble because the castle was in the charge of Lady Mary Bankes. Her husband, Sir John Bankes, was away with the king, and Lady Mary had only five elderly men and her maids in the castle. Yet when the Roundheads demanded the cannons her reply was to fire them from the battlements. The forty men took to their heels.

On 23 June a force of six hundred men under the command of Sir Walter Earle besieged Corfe. Lady Mary had expected this and had prepared for it by obtaining a large stock of food and a band of eighty men loyal to the Royalist cause. Despite their artillery the Parliamentarians made little impression on the castle and eventually news came that the Earl of Caernarvon was approaching with a force of dragoons. The attack became a rout, the Roundheads leaving behind a hundred dead and all their artillery.

Lady Mary continued to hold Corfe unmolested until the end of 1645 when the final siege took place under the command of Colonel Bingham. Once more the cannon roared and once more the defenders on the battlements managed to repulse the daily attacks with hardly any loss to themselves. Then, on 26 February 1646, an officer of the castle betrayed it in return for a promise of protection. Lady Mary surrendered, and Colonel Bingham permitted her to leave the castle with her children and dependants. She lived to see the Restoration, dying a year after the return of Charles II.

On 5 March 1646 Cromwell ordered the destruction

of Corfe. Cartloads of gunpowder were hauled up the steep slope to the castle, and then what had been one of the strongest fortresses in Britain was blasted into the state we see today.

But Cromwell's explosives did not frighten away the phantoms which still haunt the ruins. I am told by friends living in Dorset that there are a number of white figures usually seen at dusk near the castle's walls but whether they are the ghosts of King John's victims or of the men who were killed in the Civil War sieges none can say.

Hever Castle in Kent has everything for the visitor – it is a stately home complete with period furniture, works of art and a collection of medieval instruments of torture and execution. In its huge grounds there is a maze, a reconstructed Tudor village and a genuine smugglers' cave in Park Wood. It can also boast the ghost of Anne Boleyn.

Nearly four and a half centuries have passed since her execution in the Tower of London, yet her fascination as a historical character remains. The love Henry VIII felt for her led to the English Reformation, she became the mother of Elizabeth I, and her tragic death placed her among the quartet of British queens who have knelt at the headsman's block.

Work was begun on Hever Castle towards the end of the thirteenth century, and two centuries later a Tudor house was completed within its walls by Sir Thomas Boleyn, whose daughter Anne – just returned from the French court – met King Henry in the castle garden. His passion for her began in 1522, though he continued to treat his wife Queen Catherine of Aragon with suitable respect until 1527.

In order to be free of his first wife the king broke away from the Catholic Church, which did not allow divorce, and married Anne in 1533. She was crowned queen in June of that year, but before long the king began to tire of her, especially after the birth of a baby girl who was to become the future Queen Elizabeth I – Henry was desperately anxious to have a son to be heir to his throne. Soon Henry fell in love again, this time with one of his wife's maids of honour named Jane Seymour, and Queen Anne was sent to the headsman on a trumped-up treason charge which included the accusation of practising black magic.

Following her execution Anne's ghost has been seen to glide over a bridge spanning the River Eden in the castle grounds, and on each occasion the appearance of the ghost has been reported on Christmas Eve.

Henry VIII's first wife Catherine of Aragon lived in retirement after the king divorced her, spending the last two years of her life in Kimbolton Castle in Cambridgeshire where she would supervise the cooking of her food as she lived in morbid fear of being poisoned. Since her death in 1536 her ghost has frequently been glimpsed at Kimbolton and though part of the building collapsed at the beginning of the eighteenth century, the haunted Queen's Chamber remains intact.

It is surprising that Berkeley Castle in Gloucestershire does not have a royal ghost because it was here in 1327 that Edward II died when his captors thrust a red-hot spit into his body. The assassination had been carried out by the order of his wife Queen Isabella and her lover Roger Mortimer who had gained control of the kingdom after they had led an army against the unpopular king.

Today at Berkeley Castle you can see the King's Gallery where Edward was imprisoned. In one corner of the room is a hole like the opening of a well, and below it a shaft drops eight and a half metres to the level of the courtyard outside. This was the castle dungeon and putrefying carcasses of cattle were thrown into it in the hope that the stench would undermine the king's health and infect him with a pestilence so it would appear that he died of natural causes. In those days the chamber was much smaller than it is today, and the effect of the fetor in the confined space on the prisoner can be imagined. But Edward had a strong constitution and survived the charnel vapour, whereupon Roger Mortimer sent word to the king's gaolers to kill him by a more direct method.

Soon afterwards the fourteen-year-old son of the dead king and Queen Isabella became Edward III, but he soon found he was a monarch in name only – the real power remained with his mother and Roger Mortimer whom she made Earl of March. The couple retained two-thirds of England's taxes for their own use and the people began to realise that they had exchanged a weak and foolish king for a ruthless pair of tyrants.

Young Edward planned to overthrow the man who had been responsible for his father's death and who regarded him as a mere puppet, but he knew it would not be easy. Queen Isabella and Mortimer were living in Nottingham Castle protected by a fanatically loyal army of Mortimer's Welsh archers. The youth knew it would be impossible to storm the castle, which had been King John's favourite fortress. Instead he would have to strike from within. He learned that there was a secret passage running into the castle from an inn called The Trip to Jerusalem – which still boasts of being the oldest inn in England and is actually built into the base of the cliff on which the castle stands.

On the night of 19 October 1330 Sir William Eland, the deputy constable of the castle, led two dozen of Edward's most trusted companions through the tunnel and into the castle where the king was waiting for them. Silently the avenging party went to the inner ward where they burst into the queen's chamber. Ignoring his mother's cry of '*Bel fitz, eiez pitie du gentil Mortimer!*' – which was Norman French for 'Fair son, spare the gentle Mortimer!' – Edward seized the Earl of March and had him imprisoned in a dungeon in the honeycomb of passages beneath the castle. Later he was taken to London where he was found guilty of having 'murdered and killed the king's father' and soon afterwards he was

51

hanged at Tyburn. For the remaining twenty-eight years of her life Isabella was imprisoned in Castle Rising in Norfolk.

At The Trip to Jerusalem strange noises are heard in its subterranean chambers beneath Nottingham Castle. They are the sounds of regular footsteps as though someone were marching up and down in a confined space. They are believed to be the supernatural echoes of Roger Mortimer who was imprisoned close to the inn's cellars in a dungeon still known as Mortimer's Hole.

During the Second World War some American soldiers heard the disembodied voice of a woman screaming 'foreign words' above their heads at the castle. When they told local people about their experience they were informed that they had heard Queen Isabella crying yet again.

The ghost of the queen has been seen wandering in the castle's underground passages, searching for her lover who had been hidden away in the dungeon which still bears his name.

Queen Isabella also haunts the sombre ruins of Castle Rising. During her imprisonment there her grandson the Black Prince was the lord of Rising, but it seems to have made no difference to her fate. Her white form has been seen on a stone staircase within the castle, and if the ghostly bursts of maniacal laughter which have been heard resounding hideously within the shattered ramparts are anything to go by she must have lost her reason before her death in 1358.

Dacre Castle in Cumbria has been haunted by three kings who met on its site a thousand years ago. The castle is really a massive fortified tower which was built in the fourteenth century by Ranulph Dacre (who also built Naworth Castle) on the earthworks of an earlier fortification. In the eighteenth century its walls were pierced to make windows. Parts of its moat can still be seen, and one of its rooms is still known as the King's Room in memory of the historic meeting which took place so long ago.

King Athelstan had given his sister in marriage to Sithric, King of Northumbria, but the latter failed to meet his obligations to the Saxon monarch. He died before retribution could catch up with him, but his two sons, Anlaf and Guthred, were forced to flee to the court of King Constantine of Scotland. He attempted to regain Northumbria for the brothers with the aid of King Donal of Strathclyde, but their campaign failed and finally the two northern kings met Athelstan to hear his terms at the site of Dacre Castle.

The meeting was not long over when all the kingdoms of the North decided to humble the Saxon king, and to this end they were joined by the Kings of Cumbria, Wales and Ireland, and a fleet of over six hundred Danish ships which sailed into the Humber to invade Northumbria.

It seemed the Saxons would be overwhelmed by the confederation of Celts and Danes which faced them on the field of Brunanburgh, but, led by King Athelstan and his brother Edmund, they fought with such valour that they won the day. An anonymous poem in the *Anglo-Saxon Chronicle* describes their victory in words which give us a taste of the enthusiasm for war in the Dark Ages:

Then the Norsemen departed in their nailed ships, bloodstained survivors of spears, on Dingesmere over the deep water to seek Dublin, Ireland once more, sorry of heart. The two brothers likewise, king and atheling both, sought their own country, the land of the West Saxons, exulting in war. They left behind them, to joy in the carrion, the black and horn-beaked raven with his dusky plumage, and the dun-feathered eagle with his white-tipped tail, greedy hawk of battle, to take toll of the corpses. . . .

Why the shades of the three ancient kings who met before this bloody conflict should return to Dacre Castle none can say, but — through the ages which have passed since the ravens fed on their dead followers — their phantoms have continued to appear in the castle grounds.

Another castle with a royal spectre is Muncaster Castle in Cumbria, and connected with the ghost is its famous talisman known as the Luck of Muncaster. This is a bowl of green-tinted glass, decorated with purple and gold, and most probably made in Venice. It was given to the Penningtons, who owned the castle, by Henry VI in gratitude for the shelter given him when he was a fugitive during the Wars of the Roses.

A verse connected with the bowl concludes:

In Muncaster Castle good luck shall be
Till this charmed cup be broken.

The castle has two ghosts. Henry VI was put to death in the Tower of London when Edward IV seized his throne and afterwards his ghost returned to Muncaster and has been glimpsed in the room where he had hidden.

The other phantom appears minus his head. In life he was a young carpenter who forgot his humble station when he fell in love with Helwise, the daughter of Sir Ferdinand Pennington. It would have been better for the young man if the girl had not returned his love because her father had already planned marriage for her. When she refused to marry the knight of *his* choice, Sir Ferdinand was so infuriated he ordered his jester Tom the Fool to get rid of the carpenter.

The jester murdered the young man, cut off his head and took it to his master as proof of the murder. But that was not the end of the matter — since then a headless figure materialises in the castle as a silent reminder of the crime.

## Chapter 7

# Phantoms of the Round Table

Britain's two greatest legendary heroes are Robin Hood and King Arthur — I say 'legendary' because we have no proof that either of them actually existed. Yet in the case of King Arthur there are more landmarks named after him than all our historical monarchs put together — only the Devil is mentioned in more British place names. And all over the country there are places which are traditionally connected with the exploits of Arthur and the Knights of the Round Table.

I believe that the real Arthur was a Celtic leader who fought against invading Saxons. The Roman legions left Britain in AD 410 to go to the defence of Rome against her enemies and their withdrawal was followed by terrifying raids by the Angles and Saxons. The Britons retreated into Wales and Cornwall, taking with them Christianity, the religion which the Romans had given them. Among them rose a champion of their freedom and faith, and the *Cambrian Annals*, written in the tenth century, relate that the Saxons were routed by Arthur at Mount Badon in 516. They also mention the Battle of Camlan, fought in 537, at which Arthur fell.

There have been many books written about this mysterious king, but this book is about haunted castles and therefore we shall concentrate on the castles connected with ghosts who in life were part of the famous

55

Round Table fellowship. The main one is the magnificent ruin of Tintagel which crouches on a rocky headland on the Atlantic coast of Cornwall and where – according to legend – Arthur was born.

The present Tintagel Castle dates back to 1145 when it was built by Reginald, Earl of Cornwall, and as he died without an heir the castle passed through many hands – the most famous owner being the Black Prince. When it was built it was on the headland, but due to erosion by the sea part of it became an island and a bridge was constructed to join the two parts. By the end of the fifteenth century it had been allowed to decay as there seems to have been no strategic purpose left for it to fulfil.

Still to be seen are ramparts, gateways, the walls of the chapel and the Great Hall as well as the entrance to a tunnel cut in the rock which is thought to lead down to the sea. Perhaps the most dramatic sight Tintagel has to offer is Merlin's Cave which can be reached by paths winding down to the stony beach. The fact that the present castle only dates back to the twelfth century does not rule out the possibility that Arthur was associated with the site, as Celtic remains have been excavated there dating back to the fifth century.

You have only to visit Tintagel to appreciate its magical atmosphere and it is easy to believe the legend which goes back through the centuries, that the spirit of King Arthur returns periodically to his birthplace. There is anther curious local tradition that twice a year the whole castle disappears and briefly materialises in some strange fairy realm.

King Arthur's capital was called Camelot, and several places are claimed to be its site. Today the most promising one is the great Somerset prehistoric hillfort known as Cadbury Castle where excavations were begun in 1966 by the Camelot Research Committee and work continues in the hope of finding evidence which will identify it as the real Camelot. Apparently the imposing hill and its earthworks — said to be some of the finest in the country — were known locally as Camelot as late as the sixteenth century.

Cadbury Castle dominates the plain south of the A303 which runs between Wincanton and Sparkford, and tales of phantom knights who haunt it go back far in history. It was said that on Midsummer's Eve the ghost of King Arthur rides at the head of a cavalcade of spectral knights along a causeway linking the villages of North Barrow and South Barrow. The latter is directly in line with Cadbury Castle and Glastonbury where in 1191 the monks of the abbey found two bodies which they believed were those of the king and queen. A lead cross was found in the grave on which was inscribed: *'Hic jacet sepultus inclytus Rex Arthurus in Insula Avalonia* 'Here lies interred in the Isle of Avalon the renowned King Arthur.'

An old path which ran from Cadbury Castle to Glastonbury is known as King Arthur's Hunting Causeway.

On a Midsummer Eve, shortly after the First World War, a lady who lived close to Cadbury Castle was driving home with a friend at night when she noticed a string of lights moving down the great mound, and as she drove nearer these turned out to be flames illuminating the points of lances carried by a troop of mounted warriors led by a man of majestic bearing. Silently the company advanced and then it suddenly vanished.

The fact that the lances' tips appeared to be outlined with fire coincided exactly with descriptions of the knights riding between the Barrow villages.

Many of the legends about King Arthur claim that he never died of his wounds received at Camlan but that he is sleeping in a secret place with all his knights until some future time when they will awaken to come to the aid of Britain. Sites for the hidden cavern where they lie in their centuries-old trance have been given in various parts of the country and include Sewingshields Castle on Hadrian's Wall.

This was a Northumbrian border tower which stood until the close of the sixteenth century, but is now marked only by ditches and mounds. These are a little to the north of Hadrian's Wall in the Sewingshields Crags area near the fort of Brocolitia with its fascinating Mithraic Temple. The importance of Sewingshields in folklore is that it marks the site of King Arthur's Hall where he rests with his queen and court until the day someone should enter the hidden cavern and go through the ritual of blowing a horn which lies on a table at the entrance, and then with Excalibur cut a garter placed beside it.

About a hundred and sixty years ago a shepherd sat on a mound of the castle, keeping an eye on his sheep and knitting to pass the time. His ball of wool fell from his lap and rolled down a slope to disappear in a patch of briars. He followed the thread and found the ball had fallen into a hidden pit which, when he lowered himself into it, turned out to be a vaulted passage. Remembering the legend, he went forward, following the wool like Theseus following Ariadne's thread in the Minotaur's labyrinth. As the tunnel grew darker bats flitted about him and his courage ebbed. He was about to turn back when he saw a glimmer ahead.

Forcing himself to continue, he found it grew brighter until he entered a huge hall illuminated by a fire flaming from a crevice in the centre of the stone floor. By its light the intruder saw knights and ladies resting on couches ranged round the carved walls while on two thrones a king and queen slept with their heads resting in their hands. Close to them snored a pack of hounds.

True to tradition there was a table on which stood a horn, a sword and a garter. The shepherd drew the blade from its scabbard and cut the garter, and as he did so the eyes of the sleepers slowly opened and they began to sit up. In wonder the man sheathed the sword, and with this the enchantment resumed its ancient power. Eyelids fell, the knights and ladies lay back on their couches, the hounds twitched and lay still, but, before his head drooped again, the monarch declared:

'O woe betide that evil day
On which this witless wight was born,
Who drew the sword, the garter cut,
But never blew the bugle horn!'

Terror brought on a loss of memory and the next thing the shepherd knew was that he was wandering aimlessly in the remains of the castle. His wool was lost and he was never again able to locate the hole that led to the hall's entrance tunnel.

The same kind of legend is told about Dunstanburgh, the largest Northumbrian castle, whose northern boundary is a cliff which plunges a dizzy thirty metres to the restless North Sea.

To reach its great shattered gatehouse you have to walk two kilometres over rough ground from the tiny fishing village of Craster. It was built nearly seven centuries ago by Thomas Plantagenet, second Earl of Lancaster, who no doubt realised this remote coast could not be bettered as a place of refuge. He knew he was likely to need such a retreat because he devoted his life to opposing Edward II. Yet when his side lost the Battle of Boroughbridge in 1322 he refused to flee to Dunstanburgh, with the result that he was beheaded in his own castle at Pontefract.

During the Wars of the Roses, Dunstanburgh remained a stronghold for the cause of the Red Rose until the Earl of Warwick captured it with a force of ten thousand men. When the century-long power struggle ended, Dunstanburgh was in a damaged state as a result of the battering it had received during various sieges, and nothing was done to repair it. In 1538 Henry VIII's commissioners reported it to be 'very ruinous', and a splendid ruin it has remained since then.

When I visited it a custodian kindly showed me the

dungeon which lay beneath one of the gatehouse towers.

'Once they were down there they had nothing but a lick-stone,' he said, shaking his head as though still amazed at old cruelties.

'What was a lick-stone?' I asked.

'It's a piece of smooth stone set in the wall which, because of condensation, would get moist,' he explained. 'The prisoners tried to slake their thirsts by running their tongues over it. It's still down there.'

The legend behind Dunstanburgh dates from a time when the castle was already a ruin. A knight named Sir Guy was making a journey along the Northumbrian coast when the dusk was split by lightning and heavy raindrops splashed against his face. Remembering that abandoned Dunstanburgh was in the vicinity, Sir Guy spurred his horse forward in the hope of finding some shelter in the ruins. When he reached the castle he led his horse to the archway in the keep gatehouse where, with the wind screeching through jagged embrasures, he waited for the storm to pass.

Suddenly a glowing figure appeared before the knight and, in a voice which rang above the gale, it commanded him to follow if he wished to find a 'beauty bright'. Sir Guy obeyed, and the ghostly guide led him into a labyrinth beneath the castle where they finally reached a brass-bound door.

Unseen hands caused it to creak open, and the knight found himself in a huge black-draped cavern, lit by a hundred lights which flickered on a hundred armoured warriors with death-white faces who lay entranced by their sleeping warhorses. At the far end of the hall, guarded by two skeletons, was a crystal coffin, and the amazed knight could see that within it − like some Sleeping Beauty − there was a lady with tears glistening on her cheek.

One of the guardians of this transparent tomb held a

horn in his bony fingers, the other gripped a sword. The guide then told Sir Guy that he had to choose one of these objects, and that the fate of the enchanted lady and himself would depend on his choice.

Sir Guy stood for a long time trying to reason out an answer to the riddle, and it seemed logical that he should take the horn if he was to awaken the sleeper.

Summoning up his courage he seized the horn, put it to his lips and sent a high-pitched blast echoing through the subterranean chamber. At its note the horses snorted and stamped their hooves, the warriors sprang to their feet with their hands on their weapons — but as Sir Guy looked hopefully at the lady within the crystal the whole scene began to dissolve as in a nightmare. The knight felt as though he was spinning furiously while in his ears (according to an old ballad) thundered these words:

'Shame on the coward who sounded a horn
When he might have unsheathed a sword!

He awoke with the sun just climbing above the castle's ramparts, while nearby his horse restlessly pawed the weed-covered cobbles. Immediately Sir Guy began to search for the entrance to the underground maze and for the sleeping lady who had bewitched him with her serene beauty, but though he devoted years to the quest he had no more luck that the shepherd who found and lost a magical hall beneath Sewingshields Castle.

## Chapter 8

# Harbingers of Death

According to the dictionary a harbinger is one who announces the approach of something – and there are several British castles with their own harbingers which appear before death or disaster strikes the families who own them. One of the strangest of these is at Inveraray Castle in the Argyll area of Strathclyde Region. With its cone-shaped roofs rising from its battlemented towers, and unusual greenish stonework, it looks like a storybook illustration, and is the hereditary seat of the dukes of Argyll, chiefs of the Clan Campbell.

When one of these chiefs was about to die, ravens would arrive and circle about the castle, but a much more unusual omen was described by Mr H. W. Hill, once the secretary of the English Church Union, who wrote of how in 1913 he dined with Niall Campbell just after the death of his father Lord Archibald Campbell. During the meal the subject of omens came up, Mr Hill mentioning that the ominous gathering of ravens had been described in the Scottish Press.

Niall Campbell said he believed in the tradition, and added that a far more mysterious sign was the galley which sailed over Loch Fyne just prior to his father's death. This vessel, shaped like the ship which is part of the Campbell arms, had three silent figures standing on board as it sailed up the loch. It then continued its voyage *overland*, to vanish at a site associated with St Columba which had been given to the Church by the Campbells.

It was believed the galley always made this journey when the head of the clan was dying, and on the recent occasion of Lord Archibald's death it had been seen by many witnesses. Not all had the Celtic blood and the 'second sight' associated with it which is often needed to see such supernatural signs. An Englishman, seeing the galley sail over the shore of the loch, shouted, 'Look at that funny airship!'

Apart from the ravens and the galley, Inveraray Castle is haunted by a phantom harper who was executed by order of the Marquis of Montrose when he drove Lord Argyll from the castle in 1644. The ghost, which has been described as a 'harmless little old thing', appears in Campbell tartan. Apart from his harping, he makes a noise in the Green Library as though books are being flung about, yet when anyone goes to investigate the disturbance every volume is in place.

Inveraray's most sensational supernatural occurrence was a 'phantom battle' which was linked with a ghostly prophecy.

On 10 July 1758 the famous physician Sir William Hart was walking in the grounds of the castle accompanied by a friend and a servant. One of the men looked up into the sky and gave an exclamation of amazement. The other two followed his gaze and saw a battle actually taking place high above them. Many of the spectral soldiers wore the uniform of the Highlanders and they were desperately attacking a fort defended by a French garrison.

The dumbfounded watchers saw troops endeavour to scale the ramparts again and again, while the defenders poured volleys of musket fire on them. The British force seemed to be without scaling ladders and the men climbed on each other's shoulders in almost suicidal attempts to gain the top of the walls. When they finally withdrew they left the ground covered with their dead comrades. As the musket smoke ceased to roll from the French stronghold the scene of carnage dissolved and only clear summer sky remained above the castle.

Soon afterwards two ladies, the Miss Campbells of Ederin, arrived at Inveraray breathless with a tale they had to tell. They had been on the road which ran to Kilmalieu when they saw a battle in the sky and described it exactly as the three men had seen it.

There was great speculation as to what it could mean. At that time England was at war with the French in America, and it was known that the Highlanders were stationed at Albany, but the exact nature of the battle was not known until weeks later when an official bulletin stated that the Highlanders had been in action against a French fort at Ticonderoga on Lake George and had lost over three hundred men killed and as many wounded. The date of the battle was 10 July — the same date that the five people had seen its 'mirage' above the castle.

A stone chapel going up in a sheet of supernatural fire was the dramatic warning which preceded the death of the lords of Rosslyn Castle. Although the chapel appeared to blaze the flames which terrified the onlookers left no scorch marks on the ancient walls with their finely chiselled buttresses and grotesque gargoyles.

Describing the dread omen the author and poet Sir Walter Scott wrote:

Blazed battlement and pinnet high,
Blazed every rose-carved buttress fair;
So still they blaze, when fate is nigh
The lordly line of Hugh St Clair.

Today all that remains of Rosslyn Castle are creeper-covered ruins perched high above the North Esk river about twelve kilometres south of Edinburgh. It was built in the fourteenth century by Sir William St Clair, and the haunted chapel was begun in 1446. Happily the chapel did not crumble into ruins with the castle − it is a most amazing place, being decorated with extraordinary stone carvings.

Should you visit the chapel, look for the fantastically sculptured column known as the Apprentice Pillar whose carved decorations include tiny angels playing a portable organ, a whistle and an old-fashioned instrument called a tambour.

As the pillar took shape it was regarded as the finest example of stone carving in the chapel, and the chief mason felt unable to complete it without further study of his craft. He travelled to Italy to perfect his skill under a famous craftsman and while he was away a young apprentice innocently worked at the pillar. He had just completed it when his master returned.

Despite the fact that the young man's work was perfect, the mason was so furious he had not completed the work himself that he struck the apprentice on the head with his mallet, killing him on the spot. After the tragedy there was a widespread belief that the chapel was haunted and you can see the apprentice's face carved beneath a leafy frieze in the south-west corner of the building.

Rosslyn's other supernatural character is a lady who lies in a trance in a vault beneath the castle's foundations, guarding a fabulous treasure. As in similar legends, it will take the blast of a special trumpet to rouse her from her centuries-old sleep.

South of the Border England has its share of castles which have been haunted by heralds of death.

The saddest ghost you will read about in this book is that of a child, known as the Gilsland Boy. His phantom tries to make contact with the living along an area of the Roman Wall between the village of Gilsland and the remains of Triermain Castle, the first Norman castle to be built in the district.

The legend behind the Gilsland Boy is that he was the

victim of a wicked uncle who saw him as the only obstacle to inheriting Triermain when the child was orphaned. In the depth of winter, after weakening him through hunger, the man took the unhappy heir out on to snow-covered Thirlwall Common where he deliberately lost him. It was several days before the small frozen corpse was found where the child had sought shelter by a rock. But the anguish did not die with the boy — according to local legend he appeared whenever a descendant of the uncle was about to be taken ill. If the illness was to prove fatal the boy would lay his hand on the affected part and whisper:

'Cauld, cauld, aye, cauld.
An' ye'll be cauld for evermair.'

As with so many old legends, there is an alternative version in which it is not a wicked uncle that is to blame but an equally evil folktale character — the cruel stepmother. In this case she married a widowed lord of Triermain and was jealous of his only son, preferring that her future offspring should be heirs to the castle.

When her husband was away she took the opportunity to lock the child in a cellar where he was left to die of cold and starvation. But both stories agree that the boy haunts the descendants of the one who wronged him, and on the rhyme of ill omen with which he heralds their last hours.

A small, invisible and icy hand touching yours is the way the boy usually manifests himself. It is said that you will feel the coldness of his fingers through your sleeve if he tries to draw attention to his plight by seizing your arm. On rare occasions when he has actually been seen he has been described as a frightened-looking little boy with chattering teeth who stretches out his hands as though imploring food.

As I live in Gilsland I have always been interested in the boy, and by a strange coincidence I heard of two incidents connected with him while I was working on this book. The first happened when the wife of a local farmer was walking in a field close to the Roman Wall towards dusk. Suddenly she felt a small hand grip her tightly. Thinking that a child had run up behind her and taken her hand, she looked down – and saw that there was nobody there even though she could still feel small fingers clutching hers. The shock was so great that she had to spend several days in bed, and she will never go for an evening walk near the Roman Wall again.

The second incident concerned two German tourists who were driving along the road which runs parallel to the wall. Again it was dusk, and the driver switched on his lights. To his horror he saw a child standing motionless in the middle of the road. He slammed on his brakes and the car skidded to a wild halt, but in doing so the child seemed to vanish under the bonnet.

The two men leapt out. They looked under the car, fearful of what they might find, and when they saw nothing they searched the grass verges in case the body had been flung there. Nowhere could they find a trace of the child who had appeared in their headlights. In the end they drove to the nearest pub for a drink to steady their nerves. Only when they told their story and the legend of the Gilsland Boy was explained to them did they begin to realise that they had driven through a spectre.

Caister Castle in Norfolk had a harbinger of doom in the form of a ghostly coach. When death threatened a member of the family who owned the castle a huge carriage, unpleasantly like a horse-drawn hearse, swayed up to the castle as fast as the headless driver could urge his horses. After passing through the gates as though they were not there, it circled the courtyard several times before vanishing in the direction from which it had come.

The appearance of this prophetic vehicle went back to when the castle was owned by the Fastolf family. It had been built in 1435 by John Fastolf with money he obtained by ransoming a French knight when campaigning in France with Henry V. The unusual thing about it was that Sir John chose brick as its building material, and today Caister has claim to being one of the oldest edifices built of this material in England.

When the Pastons inherited the castle in 1459 they also inherited the prophetic coach, which would appear mysteriously before a death in the family.

In Staffordshire the ruins of Chartley Castle near Uttoxeter recall the strange haunting of the Ferrars family who occupied it from the time of the Conquest. They bred a special herd of cattle which were distinguished by the fact that they were white with reddish ears − a herd which lasted until the beginning of this century. When one of the cows gave birth to a black calf it meant that a head of the family would soon die, an omen which seems to have been proved true on several occasions. A black calf would provoke no horror now − the tenth earl, having no heir, sold the estate.

Leeds Castle, which frowns over a lake near Maidstone in Kent, is famous for possessing Anne Boleyn's shoes, England's oldest pendulum clock − and a phantom hound whose appearance bodes ill for those who live within its walls. Perhaps it dates back to 1431 when Henry VI's aunt, Eleanor of Gloucester, was found guilty of having practised 'necromancy, witchcraft, heresy and treason', and was imprisoned in the castle for the rest of her life.

It is an old belief at Arundel Castle, on the south coast, that when one of the family is about to die a strange white bird is seen fluttering desperately against the panes of one of the windows.

The castle − home of the Dukes of Norfolk and their ancestors for over seven centuries − is one of the show-places of Britain. It has often been described as a

Windsor Castle on a smaller scale, complete with a round keep, upper and lower baileys, and stone steps protected by battlemented walls leading up to the keep.

Work began on the castle during the reign of Edward the Confessor on the high ground on the bank of the River Arun, although it was not until William I gave the fortress to his relative, Roger Montgomery, that stone began to replace its timber construction. One of Roger's sons, Earl Robert, rebelled against Henry I who besieged the castle in 1102, and the fact that the castle was able to hold out for twelve weeks against the royal army indicated its strength.

In the Civil War Parliamentarian forces besieged Arundel for eighteen days, bombarding it with a cannon placed in the tower of St Nicholas's church. The marks of its cannonballs are still to be seen on the walls of the barbican towers.

Cromwell's artillery sounded the death knell for castles as places of military importance, and Arundel was allowed to remain a ruin until 1716 when the eighth Duke of Norfolk began to restore it. This work was carried on by his descendants until today Arundel stands in its former glory.

Apart from the mysterious white bird, Arundel has its share of ghosts, including the silvery shape of a young girl sometimes seen in moonlight near one of the towers from which she threw herself as the result of an unhappy love affair.

Another ghost, the Blue Man, has appeared in the library bending over an old book. Dressed in a blue costume from the time of Charles II, he seems to be seeking some piece of information which he can never find.

In the kitchen, during the dead of night, there is sometimes heard the rattle of pots and pans — the sound of a scullion hard at work. It is a supernatural echo going back two centuries to when a kitchen lad was brutally treated there. From time to time a more impressive sound booms from the past, the thunder of the Parliamentarian artillery which pounded the castle walls during the Christmas siege of 1643.

White owls were harbingers to the Arundells of Wardour Castle near Salisbury. Its most stirring time was during the Civil War when Lord Arundell went to fight for the king, leaving his wife Blanche to hold the castle with a handful of retainers. An army of thirteen hundred Roundheads besieged it in May 1643, and for five days Lady Blanche held out with her twenty-five defenders. Food and shot soon ran out. Two mines were exploded under the walls, and after five days the gates were opened in surrender.

Wardour now became a Parliamentary garrison. Lord Arundell died and his successor returned to Wardour with a small force and recaptured it, after which the family lived in the undamaged corn store until a new castle was built over a century later.

Not only white owls haunted the family – a spectre of Lady Blanche Arundell appeared in the castle as the real woman did when she loaded the matchlock guns of her men during the famous siege. The family died out over thirty years ago, but the phantom of Lady Blanche has still been glimpsed as dusk thickens about the ruins.

*Chapter 9*

# Fairies and Enchantment

Above the sound of a flooded stream rushing against its rocky banks comes the beat of hooves on wet, heather-covered ground, and through the swirling mist material-ises the outline of a horseman. *But as it becomes clearer it can be seen that the figure crouching desperately over the neck of the galloping steed is without a head!*

This terrifying spectre is known as Ewan of the Little Head and he can be glimpsed racing between Loch Squabain and Moy Castle on the Isle of Mull.

The story began with the marriage of the heir of the Maclaine chief who held Moy Castle whose square ruins still stand at the head of Loch Buie. When the wedding celebrations were over Ewan took his bride from his father's stronghold to the hall he had established on a tiny island in Loch Squabain, once the site of a pre-historic fortification. The ambitious lady was far from satisfied with this arrangement, criticising her new home in comparison with the larger and more comfortable Moy Castle. Her discontent began to infect Ewan who complained to his father that he was not properly housed for a man in his position.

Old Maclaine would shrug and tell his son to be patient, pointing out that before long he would inherit Moy. But the spark of discontent, cunningly fanned by Ewan's wife, flared into a quarrel between the chief and his son, the former bitterly resenting the way his heir hungered for his inheritance, the latter full of complaint that his father had not provided properly for him.

Tension mounted between Maclaine and his clansmen at Moy and Ewan and his followers at Loch Squabain until blows were exchanged, thus starting a family feud.

One evening, as Ewan was walking towards the shore of Loch Squabain, he saw an old woman bending over a brook washing shirts, and felt his blood chill because he knew she was a Bean-nighe, one of the terrible fairy washerwomen who were sometimes found beside a stream scrubbing the bloodied shirts of those destined to be killed in battle. A Bean-nighe was not hard to recognise because she had such long breasts that she hung them back over her shoulders as she bent over her ill-omened work. If a man saw her and wanted to know the future he should creep up behind her, lay hold of one of her breasts and declare that he was her foster son.

The fairy would then answer any question put to her, the usual one being the names of the doomed men whose shirts she was washing. If a garment belonged to an enemy the Bean-nighe would continue with her washing, but if it belonged to her new 'son' she could be persuaded to stop.

Ewan went through the traditional procedure but it seemed the fairy had gone too far with her fateful work, though she had a crumb of comfort for him. She explained that although his shirt was among those of tomorrow's victims, he might be spared if on the following morning his wife gave him a generous lump of butter at breakfast without his telling her to do so.

One can imagine the state of Ewan's feelings next day when he sat at table in his island castle and waited for his wife to give him his food. As might be expected from a lady whose ambition had sparked off a family feud, she was not very interested in housekeeping, and she told her husband he would have to eat his bread dry as she had run out of butter.

Knowing that there was no way of escaping his destiny, Ewan led his men from Loch Squabain to meet a raiding party of his father's retainers, and in the fighting which followed his head was struck from his shoulders.

Not all Scottish fairies are as doom-laden as the Bean-nighe, and there are fairylike women known as Glaistigs or Elle maids who are often very helpful. The Glaistig is in fact a mortal who has been endowed with fairy attributes, and like true fairies she wears a green dress has the power of instant invisibility. But she can be recognised for what she is because her face is grey — her name coming from the word '*glas*', meaning 'grey'. Her role is to act as a guardian of a special site, attaching herself to a family and acting as a sort of supernatural servant.

Perhaps the best-known Glaistig was the one who attached herself to the Campbell family in Dunstaffnage Castle which overlooks the entrance to Loch Etive. It was the home of the Scottish kings before they took their Coronation Stone (now in Westminster Abbey) to Scone in the ninth century. The castle was enlarged in the thirteenth century when Alexander II was planning to attack the Viking-held Hebrides. In 1308 it was captured by Robert the Bruce after which it was entrusted to the Campbell Clan. Later — in 1746 — it became the prison of Flora Macdonald after she had helped Bonnie Prince Charlie to escape.

The Glaistig at Dunstaffnage followed the tradition of her kind by associating herself closely with the fortunes of the Campbells, often breaking into cries of joy or sorrow when good or ill fortune came to them. She was said to have watched over generation after generation until the castle was gutted by fire in 1810.

Since then the castle has been uninhabited but the Glaistig may still be there because, according to an old authority on Scottish folklore, a Glaistig would remain in a place 'after a change of tenants, even after the building was deserted and had become a nesting place for wild birds . . . her real attachment was to the building or site and when the house was to be levelled, even though the family remained on the land and a new house on another site was built, the Glaistig made a lamentable outcry and was never seen again.'

Another Scottish castle famous for its association with a fairy is Dunvegan Castle on the Isle of Skye. To reach it from Portree you have to cross the ancient Fairy Bridge which has a strong supernatural reputation. It used to be claimed that no horse could be ridden or led across it without it plunging out of control because of invisible influences.

According to the legend of Dunvegan one of the members of the MacLeod clan, who owned the castle, married a fairy woman. The couple were perfectly happy until the husband became an old man while his wife remained like a young girl — fairies do not age as fast as humans. At last the time came for her to return to her own folk and she said a sad farewell to her mortal husband at the Fairy Bridge.

Here she gave him a final present — a flag which could bestow up to three wishes. To obtain a wish a member of the clan merely had to wave it, and twice this has been done to summon supernatural help. The first time was in 1490 at the Battle of Glendale and the second in 1580 at Trumpan. On both occasions the MacLeods were granted victory. There is one wish left, and I wonder if it will ever be invoked.

As well as being able to bring aid to the clan when it is desperately needed, the flag is said to draw shoals of herrings into Dunvegan Loch when it is unfurled. If you should visit the castle you can see this rare fairy relic on display in the Fairy Room in the sixteenth-century South Tower which is a place of pilgrimage for members of the MacLeod clan from all over the world.

The family who owned Caerphilly Castle in Wales was

once plagued by a dreaded Gwrach-y-rhibyn, the hag-like fairy who put in an appearance when disaster was about to take place.

Now an impressive ruin, the castle is one of the largest British castles, covering over twelve hectares. It is certainly the largest in Wales, and is a splendid example of water and earthworks combined as a defence. Two lakes were dammed so it would be surrounded by a huge expanse of moat. Probably built on the site of a Roman fort, the first castle was begun in 1268 by Gilbert de Clare, Earl of Gloucester and Hertford and Lord of Glamorgan, but destroyed two years later. Today's castle dates from 1271 and its most unusual feature is a shattered tower which leans at a seemingly impossible angle. There are several stories as to how it came about and the one I like best is that describing how when the castle was being besieged in 1326 by forces of Queen Isabella, estranged wife of Edward II, the defenders beat back attacks by pouring molten lead from the battlements of the tower. In the end the queen's troops managed to capture it, after which they allowed water from the moat to flow into the cellar where furnaces heated the cauldrons of lead, causing a steam explosion which blasted the tower apart.

Even after the original owners, the de Clares, left the castle and it fell into disrepair, the Gwrach-y-rhibyn still appeared there when a descendant of the family was on the point of death. The ill-omened apparition always rose from a piece of swampy ground near the great moat from which she glided towards the castle walls where she disappeared.

Pennard Castle, whose ruins overlook Three Cliffs Bay south-west of Swansea, was also the haunt of a Gwrach-y-rhibyn. The ghastly apparition was last seen around the middle of the last century, but why it should return there is a mystery as the family it had attached itself to died out in the sixteenth century.

*

It was 'a dark Woman of the wild Land in the West' who brought a terrible enchantment to Bamburgh Castle on the wave-swept coast of Northumberland, but it also has a conventional ghost — a knight who appears in the massive twelfth-century keep. His figure has been described as grey and indistinct, but the fact that he is wearing armour is apparent from the clash of harness and the metallic stamp of his footstep — he is in fact a clanking ghost.

Bamburgh has been a stronghold since pre-Roman times when it was held by the Votadini tribe. It was occupied by the Romans, and after the legions returned to Rome it became the capital of the kingdom of Bernicia under the Saxon king Ida. King Ethelfrith, the grandson of Ida, married Bebba and the fortress became known as Bebbanburgh, and later Bamburgh.

It has seen the whole spectrum of English history — the setting up of Aidan's monastery on nearby Lindisfarne in 634, raids by the Norsemen in the ninth century and rebellion against the hated William II, called the Red King because of his fiery complexion. Then its lord was Robert de Mowbray, Earl of Northumberland, who was captured when the castle was besieged by royal troops. King William took the fettered earl within sight of the battlements and sent a message to the earl's lady, who still held the castle, that unless she had the gates opened she would see her husband's eyes gouged out. Bamburgh surrendered.

The Scots also besieged the castle, during the unhappy reign of King Stephen, breaching a wall and slaughtering over a hundred of the garrison. During the reign of King John the castellan had a profitable sideline in piracy, preying on coastal vessels. Like Dunstanburgh it was besieged by Yorkists during the Wars of the Roses. By now a new weapon was ending the supremacy of castles — the cannon. In the siege of 1464 Edward IV was so sorry to see artillery used on such a fine fortress that he warned the Lancastrian defenders that for every shot fired one of them would pay with his head when it fell. In June of that year, after the Red Rose was defeated at the Battle of Hexham, Bamburgh became the first castle in England to surrender to the power of gunpowder.

After this the castle was allowed to deteriorate, and later was handed over to a charity run by Dr John Sharp, the curate of the village of Bamburgh, who, having seen so many ships wrecked off the treacherous coast, started a lifeboat service. Thus the castle became Britain's first life-boat station, but the most spectacular rescue to take place before its towers happened in 1838 when Grace Darling and her father rowed out through a gale from their lighthouse on the Farne Islands to rescue survivors from the wrecked steamship *Forfarshire*. If you visit Bamburgh, it is worth spending a little time at the Grace Darling Museum in the town.

In the castle you can see a delightful old painting which tells the story of the enchanted dragon once known with terror as the Laidley Worm of Spindlestone Heugh — the Spindlestone being a natural pillar of weatherworn rock which towers close to the castle. According to the story a long time ago the elderly widowed King of Northumbria married 'a dark Woman of the wild Land in the West' who was a secret enchantress.

To make sure that there would be a great welcome for his new queen, the king sent a messenger ahead to Bamburgh to organise a splendid feast. As the royal cavalcade reached the castle, the main gate swung open and Margaret, the king's eighteen-year-old daughter, ran out to kiss her father and meet her new stepmother.

'The Queen greeted her with kisses and a smiling Face,' says the lettering surrounding the painting. 'But she was really jealous of her beauty and soon determined to be rid of so dangerous a rival.'

One day she invited the princess to her chamber, saying that she wanted to show her some jewels, but once the girl was in the room the Dark Woman bewitched her, changing her into a hideous dragonlike creature which fled wailing from the castle.

The unwilling dragon made her lair among the crags by Spindlestone Heugh and, unable to control her new nature, became the terror of the district by carrying off sheep and cattle to devour. The fame of the Laidley Worm, as the dragon was called, reached a knight known as Childe Wynd — 'childe' being an old word for a youth of noble birth. With his companions he set off in a boat to Bamburgh, but the dragon was waiting for them on the shore. Her fiery breath prevented them from beaching their craft so they sailed on to Budle Bay where they landed safely.

Seeing this, the worm retreated and Childe Wynd outdistanced his men as he ran after the beast and overtook it among the Spindlestone crags. Raising his sword to strike in the approved St George style, he held back the blow when tears began to flow from the monster's huge eyes. Sheathing his blade, the knight listened while the Laidley Worm told him her story and explained that the enchantment could be reversed if he would plant three kisses on her hideous lizardlike face before the sun went down behind the castle.

Summoning up all his courage, Childe Wynd walked up to the ferocious-looking creature and did as he was asked. The bright scales of the dragon dimmed, the tremendous body began to shrink and the knight had to leap back as it suddenly burst into flames. When the smoke swirled away he saw a beautiful girl standing on the ashes of her former self. Wrapping her in his cloak, he took her to Bamburgh Castle where the old king was overjoyed by the removal of the Laidley Worm's menace and the return of his daughter. In the best fairy-tale tradition he offered Princess Margaret in marriage to the knight who had been brave enough to free her from her enchantment.

Because Childe Wynd had broken the spell, it

with the result that she was transformed into a speckled toad.

A Bamburgh legend tells that the creature still squats in a hidden cavern in the foundations beneath the castle and, as with the Laidley Worm, it is still possible for the enchantment to be lifted. Once every seven years the door of the cavern opens magically in case a hero wants to prove his bravery by releasing the Dark Woman from her bewitchment. All he would have to do is enter the dismal cave, unsheath Childe Wynd's sword three times, blow three ringing blasts on his horn and then press the toad against his lips.

## Chapter 10

# Ghostly Echoes

Glimmering knights, headless ladies and strange phantasms heralding doom are what one expects from British haunted castles, but some are haunted by sound — by echoes of past people or events surviving death and time.

When William the Conqueror landed at Pevensey Bay in October 1066 he brought with him prefabricated wooden forts. The Bayeux Tapestry shows that one was taken to Hastings and erected on a hastily raised mound known as a 'motte' (a prominent part of the castle today), and thus the first Norman castle was built in Britain. Three years later the land around Hastings was granted to Robert, Count of Eu, who replaced the wooden fort with a stone castle, within the walls of which a church was built.

The castle was of great importance as Hastings was the port of embarkation for Normandy, an English possession until King John lost it in 1204. Twelve years later, afraid that the French might invade and use the coastal castles as bases, he ordered Hastings Castle to be temporarily dismantled. Towards the end of that century there was a series of freak storms which finished Hastings as a port, after which the castle lost its military character but continued as a religious centre.

The haunting sound of Hastings Castle goes back to

The Tower of London – the White Tower

Windsor Castle

Hermitage Castle, in the Border country

Glamis Castle, Tayside

Corfe Castle, Dorset

The dungeon in Berkeley Castle, Gloucestershire

Arthur's court watching a tournament from the walls of Camelot –
manuscript from the Bibliothèque Royale Albert Premier, Brussels

The Apprentice Pillar in the chapel at Rosslyn Castle, near Edinburgh

Caerphilly Castle in Wales, showing the leaning tower on the left

Bamburgh Castle, Northumberland

Herstmonceux Castle, Sussex

Dover Castle, Kent, by moonlight

The Great Hall, Warwick Castle, showing some of the armour
displayed there

those days, being the swell of organ music which is sometimes heard issuing from the ruins of the castle church. But much more frightening sounds have echoed from the dungeons which were hewn out of the part of the castle known as the Mount. To reach them you must go down a flight of steps and along a suitably eerie passage. As you have probably guessed, the ghostly echoes here are the clank of chains and the moans of hungry prisoners.

The castle also has a visual ghost, said to be that of Thomas à Becket who was once a dean of the Church college there. He appears within the grounds of the castle on autumnal evenings – perhaps he is listening for the phantom organ.

There is a tradition that when the sun is bright but mist covers the sea, a replica of the castle is occasionally glimpsed as though floating on the horizon. This could be explained as a mirage, except that the sea castle is not in a ruined state – it appears as it must have been in its heyday, with banners billowing above its towers.

Taunton Castle in Somerset has several ghostly manifestations to its credit, two of them being sounds that have lingered on from the past. The castle, which was built on the site of a Saxon earthwork fortification in the twelfth century, now houses the Somerset County Museum and the Castle Hotel. It is in the hotel section that the wild strains of a fiddle have woken some guests staying in what is known as the Fiddler's Room.

In the museum section of the castle visitors have heard a tramping sound as though made by the boots of invisible soldiers. Both hauntings are thought to go back to the time of the Monmouth Rebellion, which left a remarkable number of ghosts in its wake.

On 20 June 1685 the rebel Duke of Monmouth was proclaimed James II by his Protestant followers at Taunton. That night his lieutenants celebrated the occasion with a revel at the castle. Ladies, enthusiastic for his cause, danced through the night with

Monmouth's officers. It was the last time they were to celebrate, because a few days later the duke attempted to surprise a 2700-strong royal army on Sedgemoor with a peasant army of almost the same size.

Cannon cut ghastly avenues through the ranks of the untrained rebels, and soon the attack became a horrifying shambles. Two days later the duke was caught near Ringwood and taken before his uncle, King James, where he grovelled at the royal feet and even offered to change his religion in return for a pardon. The king, gloating over this spectacle, sent him to the Tower where he was beheaded on 15 July.

This was not enough for the king who was determined to make a terrible example of all those who had supported the duke, and for his revenge he sent the ruthless Judge Jeffreys down to the West Country.

The judge opened his Bloody Assize at Winchester on 25 August 1685, when he tried Lady Alice Lisle for sheltering two rebel fugitives and sentenced her to be burned at the stake – a sentence which the king in his mercy changed to beheading. The ghost of this martyred lady still returns to the Eclipse Inn at Winchester from whose first-storey window she stepped bravely on to the scaffold.

In Taunton Jeffreys conducted the Bloody Assize in the great hall of the castle, sentencing over two hundred local men to the gibbet and condemning many more to be sold into slavery. The women who, such a short while ago, had danced gaily with Monmouth's lieutenants, were whipped.

Today the music in the Fiddler's Room is believed to go back to the merry night of Monmouth's proclamation, while the tramp of feet is that of the soldiers who dragged in the rebels to face the wrath of the the Hanging Judge.

Two visible ghosts also haunt Taunton Castle. One is of a man dressed as a cavalier and holding a pistol who appears on a certain landing. The other is of a young lady dressed in the fashion popular at the time of Monmouth's Rebellion.

The spectre of Judge Jeffreys haunts the Devon castle of Lydford, which was built at the end of the twelfth century. During the reign of Henry VIII it was described as 'one of the most heinous, contagious and detestable places in the realm' — certainly a suitable setting for the merciless Jeffreys. He has for company the ghost of Lady Howard, who for some unknown reason is said to appear as a dark hound.

The sad sounds of sighs and moaning sometimes fill the staircase which leads to the Tower Room at Tamworth Castle in Staffordshire. These echoes from the castle's past are so strong that they have been recorded on tape.

The castle, which is regarded as one of the most important in the Midlands, stands on a high motte, the keep having been built after the Conquest by the Marmion family, who were the Royal Champions of England. Previously on the castle's site was a convent built by Ethelfleda, the daughter of Alfred the Great, and perhaps the sad sighing goes back to the days when Robert de Marmion turned out the nuns. There is a legend that when this happened the phantom of Ethelfleda attacked him and gave him a wound which would not stop bleeding until he promised to allow them to return.

Today the castle belongs to the Corporation of Tamworth, and in its museum there is a fine collection of Saxon coins from the Tamworth mint. There are playgrounds and swimming pools in the grounds which were once haunted by a White Lady who had watched while Sir Lancelot slew her lover in a knightly duel.

For our next group of sound-haunted castles we must go north to the haunted Border.

Neville's Castle, which once guarded the western approach to Durham, has a curious superstition attached to it. After a Scottish army was defeated in the area in October 1346, King David II of Scotland was held prisoner at the castle. Following this a belief grew up that if you walked nine times round its walls and then knelt and pressed your ear to the ground you would hear the din of the battle in which the king was captured.

At Coupland Castle, north-west of Wooler in Northumberland, there is a room which has been haunted by the spectre of a girl who threw herself from the battlements while in a state of depression over an unhappy love affair. She was known as the White Woman, and about fifty years ago she was heard crying while the owner of the castle was away on holiday.

On his return members of the staff reported that they had heard the anguished cries of the ghost. At first the owner scoffed at them, saying that what they had heard must have been the moaning of the wind in the chimney. But he was not to remain a sceptic for long. That night he heard the wail of an unearthly voice 'half-human, half-animal'. He was considerably shaken by his experience, but more was to follow. There was a tremendous sound of footsteps moving as though inspired by some terrible panic, and described as sounding 'like a hundred people running to and fro'. The climax of the manifestation came when the owner's son saw the figure of the White Woman take shape close to the staircase.

A more unusual occurrence actually affected the building of Callaly Castle in Northumberland. When the first castle was started by the Clavering family in the reign of Henry II, on the north bank of a small river which runs into the River Aln, there was a mysterious interference. At the end of each day the masons would see their work collapse, while a voice boomed:

'Callaly Castle stands on a height,
Up in the day and down in the night,
Set it up on the shepherd's straw,
Then it will stand and fall no more.'

The builders took the disembodied advice and began work on a new castle south of the river on a site still known as Castle Hill. The foundations of the unfinished castle are still to be seen.

The second castle was later to have uncanny noises of its own.

At the turn of the century a member of the local Society of Antiquities visited the castle which was then the home of Major A. H. Browne. Mrs Browne told him that in the older part of the castle, which had been the Claverings' pele tower, there was a room with a walled doorway. While Major Browne was on a holiday in India she had taken the opportunity to have the brickwork removed and had found the room to be empty. She was convinced that in opening the sealed room she had unknowingly allowed a ghost known as the 'Wicked Priest' to escape, for ever since there had been strange noises echoing through the castle.

'Sometimes they are so loud you would think the house was being blown down,' she declared. 'There are tramplings along the passages and noises in some of the bedrooms.'

The visitor concluded: 'Mrs Browne showed me the chamber, which was close to the roof. Probably it was one of those priest's hiding holes of post-Reformation times.'

Another Northumbrian castle which has been plagued by unexplainable sounds is Wallington Hall, near Cambo. It was begun as a proper medieval castle but in 1688 Sir William Blackett built a hall on its site. You can still see some of the original cellars from which come strange sounds as though some invisible person were unpacking a crate. Stranger supernatural noises heard at Wallington are the sounds of unseen wings beating against a window and the rasp of heavy breathing in one of the bedrooms.

## Chapter 11

# Cursed Castles

'By all the demons of hell, I curse you,' screamed the wild-looking gypsy woman at the man in knight's armour and his sneering men-at-arms. Behind them two bodies dangled from a gallows set high on the wall of Edzell Castle. The woman — the mother of the two youths who had just been executed — turned to where the mistress of the castle stood white-faced.

'You, Lady Crawford, you shall not see the sun set!' she cried. 'You, Lord Crawford, you shall die a death that would make the boldest man ever born of a woman — even to witness it — shriek with fear!'

With blows and oaths Lord Crawford's retainers drove the woman away, but her curse seemed to hang over the castle for the rest of the day. The servants crossed themselves as they looked up and saw the two corpses turning in the wind, having been left on the hangman's ropes as a warning to others who would dare to poach game on the Edzell estate. But neither of these victims of the gallows had been able to speak out in their own defence — both had been dumb from birth.

When the sun went down in a crimson glory which to the superstitious seemed more like a sea of blood, Lady Crawford began to shiver with a fever. She took to her bed, and though a great fire was lit in her chamber, and leeches were applied to bleed her — a favourite remedy in those days — she died just before the chapel bell tolled midnight.

It was not long afterwards that the cruel Lord Crawford was out hunting. In chasing the game the party split up and suddenly he found that he was alone in a forest glade. But he was not alone for long. Out of the trees slunk a pack of wolves, circling the lonely man who realised that the second part of the gypsy's curse was about to be fulfilled. . . . A few moments later they sprang upon him and devoured him alive.

The ruins of Edzell Castle, which are close to the Tayside village of Edzell, retain nothing of ancient cruelty and the curse. All is peaceful now and it is a delightful spot to visit, especially the 'pleasance', or pleasure ground, which dates back to the beginning of the seventeenth century and which is surrounded by walls covered with extraordinary carvings.

A happier legend connected with Edzell concerns a lady of the castle who, after a period of illness, fell into a trance. Her physician mistook this for death and her sorrowing relatives laid her to rest in the family vault which was attached to the south side of the nearby kirk.

Hearing that she had been buried wearing her jewellery, the sexton entered the crypt at the dead of night and prised the lid off her coffin. The pale lantern light shone on the calm features of the lady and gleamed on the gold of her ornaments which he plucked from her until only her rings were left. Unable to pull them from the rigid fingers, he drew his knife and made a clumsy attempt to cut them off.

According to an old record the supposed corpse stirred, sat up and murmured 'Alas!' — though I think she probably used a more forthright expression. At this the grave-robber fainted, collapsing beside the coffin.

The lady struggled to her feet and then, holding the lantern in her bleeding hand, revived the sexton and led him out into the welcome night air. She was so thankful to be restored that she told the trembling man that if he would go with her to the castle her husband would reward him. Shrewdly guessing the sort of reward he would receive, the man begged her permission to emigrate — which he did that night.

If it had not been for his greed there might have been a White Lady haunting Edzell today.

It was a curse which brought about the downfall of Inverquharity Castle whose haunted ruins lie on private property near Kirriemuir in Tayside Region. It used to be the stronghold of wicked Sir John Ogilvie who was filled with a mad anger when a girl made it clear that she was not interested in him. She was the daughter of John White, the local miller, and Sir John, in revenge for being scorned, had him hanged in front of his family.

The village priest prayed that God would punish the evildoer, and his supplication was answered when a voice echoed through the parish church:

'The God of Heaven has heard your prayer,
He loves your zeal and verity,
To-day, you'll from your holy chair
Curse John of Inverquharity.'

The priest intoned the rite of excommunication and Sir John, who was hunting, fell from his mount and was killed instantly. From then on his ghostly visitations at the castle were so terrible that it had to be abandoned.

Ashintully Castle, a private castle east of Kirkmichael in Tayside Region, was cursed by a tinker just before he was executed for wandering unlawfully on the estate. As the noose was placed round his neck he damned to extinction the ruthless Spaldings who owned the castle, with the result that the family died out within a generation.

The phantom of the tinker is sometimes seen in the avenue of trees where he was hanged, as is another Spalding victim known as Crooked Davie. Green Jean is

Ashintully's third ghost, who wanders in the castle's private graveyard, unable to rest after an uncle had killed her so he could claim her inheritance.

In England the strangest curse on record concerns a witch and a dragon, and it was pronounced when the heir to Lambton Castle found he was unable to fulfil a vow.

Early in the fifteenth century the eldest son of the Lambton family, which had been described as 'so brave they feared neither man nor God', was fishing on the River Wear on a Sunday — something that was regarded as ungodly in those days. All morning he had sat on the bank without a bite and was so disgusted with his luck that he distressed people on their way to church with foul oaths.

At last his rod bowed and he began to pull in his line, the weight of which made him believe that he had caught a remarkably large fish, but when he hauled his catch out of the water he found a repulsive snakelike creature dangling from the hook. With a cry of disgust he wrenched it free and threw it into a nearby well where it threshed about in the clear water.

A passer-by came up as Lambton was watching it and the young heir, remarking that he seemed to have caught the Devil, asked the stranger what he thought it was. The man answered that it was like a giant newt, but that it had nine holes on each side of its mouth and this in his opinion was a sign of evil.

Some time afterwards young Lambton rode off to the Crusades in search of adventure and was away seven years, during which time the newtlike creature grew and grew until the Worm Well — as it was now called — could no longer accommodate it. It had become an enormous serpent and when it found the well too cramped it moved to a spot, about a mile away from Lambton Castle, on the north side of the Wear. Here it continued to grow so rapidly that it was able to wind itself three times round a small hill which for many generations showed the marks

of its coils, and which is still known as the Worm Hill —
'*worm*' or '*wyrm*' being the Old English word for a
dragon.

The monster terrorised the countryside, carrying off
cattle and sheep and destroying crops with its fiery
breath. Several knights rode forth to slay it in the approved style of St George, but they had little chance for
the worm was a magical creature. If they managed to
hack it in two by sword or battle-axe, the severed parts
immediately joined together again.

When young Lambton returned battle-hardened from
the Holy Land he was horrified to learn of the destruction caused by the creature which he had introduced into
the Lambton Castle estate and he was determined to
make amends by destroying it. Having heard of its magical character, he first consulted a wise woman. The witch
told him to have razors welded to his armour both back
and front, and declared that if he would vow to kill the
first living thing he met after slaying the worm she could
guarantee him victory. If he failed to keep his word a
curse would fall on the castle so that 'the lords of
Lambton for nine generations should not die in their
beds'.

Lambton readily agreed, having quickly thought how
he could fulfil his oath without endangering anybody.
The razors were attached to his armour, and before he
went to confront the worm he told his old father that as
soon as he killed it he would signal with three blasts on
his horn. At this, his favourite greyhound was to be
released so it would run to him and he could kill it, thus
fulfilling his strange promise.

The knight then walked out from the castle and
followed the river bank to where the worm was curled
round its hill. Lambton struck it with his sword, but it
had no other effect than to enrage the beast. It uncoiled
itself and proceeded to wrap its scaly body round the
young man, but the tighter it squeezed the deeper the
razors cut into it.

Badly wounded, the worm relaxed its coils and fell back exhausted, but as soon as it did so the terrible gashes in its body were healed by its sorcery. Revitalised, it once more attacked the knight.

Seeing he was not going to conquer his enemy this way, Lambton waded into the river. The worm followed him, once again wrapping its body about him. This time the cunning of the knight overcame it, for as soon as the razors cut pieces out of the creature they were carried away by the swift current. The worm, unable to renew itself, died after it had stained the Wear with its blood.

When the knight returned to the bank he blew three times on his horn. Overcome by the joy of hearing that his son still lived, the father forgot the plan to let the dog go first and ran from the castle to greet him. Thus he became the first living thing that Lambton encountered.

The knight had unbuckled his deadly armour, and when he saw his father he embraced him, then blew the horn once more and this time a servant let loose the greyhound. Lambton regretfully stabbed it as it jumped up to lick him. Nevertheless he had broken his oath – he had not killed the first living creature which had come to meet him. As a result the curse fell on the family and tradition has it that for nine generations not one of its lords died in bed. In *Vicissitudes of Families* Sir Bernard Burke states that a tradition traces the curse to one Robert Lambton who died childless in 1442, leaving his lands to his brother Thomas and a hundred marks to his brother John Lambton, Knight of Rhodes.

The ruined bulk of Hylton Castle looms above a housing estate five kilometres west of Sunderland, and like Lambton Castle, it is close to the River Wear. All that remains of the fortress built by William de Hylton in the fifteenth century is a keep gatehouse, surmounted by four turrets. Of particular interest to visitors from the United States is the so-called Washington Shield carved over the gate which depicts stars and stripes.

Once the castle was the home of a brownie — not a junior Girl Guide but a domestic elf. A folk tale tells that servants, tired of his nightly pranks in the kitchen, got rid of him by leaving out a little green cloak and hood. At midnight the brownie appeared, dressed himself in his clothes and pranced about the kitchen. He was so delighted that he forgot that he should be gone by dawn until he heard a cock crow and then he knew it was too late. Sadly he cried out:

'Here's a cloak and here's a hood,
The Cauld Lad o' Hylton will do no more good.'

The name of the brownie — the Cauld Lad — seems to have been passed on to a youth who was murdered in the castle and whose ghost laid a curse upon it. His real name was Robert Skelton, and he was employed as a groom. One day fiery Sir Robert Hylton ordered him to the stables to saddle up his horse — and to be quick about it! Minutes passed, and the impatient knight went to the stables where he saw Skelton dawdling at his work. In a fury Hylton killed him, then hid the body under straw until it was safe to take it out and throw it into a pond.

In July of that year a coroner's inquest was held on Skelton at which Sir Robert Hylton was accused of murdering the groom with a scythe. He was tried and found guilty, but by September he had received a pardon, probably because no body was produced as evidence. But from then on the curse of the Cauld Lad plagued the Hyltons.

The crash of doors being slammed or crockery being broken by an unseen hand resounded through the castle, and trees on the estate would suddenly shake violently in a phantom wind while those around them were still. Such an atmosphere of terror filled the room in which the boy had slept that none dared to enter it.

The haunting of the Hyltons continued until 1703 when the pond by the castle was drained and the skeleton of a youth was found in the mud at the bottom.

Following the discovery the last of the Hyltons died, and the curse of the Cauld Lad was lifted from the castle.

The previous castles — or their owners — all suffered retribution as a result of curses, but Sherborne Castle in Dorset had a Church curse laid on it to prevent it passing into lay hands. The site was given to Osmund, later the Bishop of Sarum, after the Conquest, and a castle was erected on a hill there after 1107. Later there was a dispute over ownership in which the then bishop challenged the Earl of Salisbury to combat to decide the question.

The matter was finally settled without violence, but to ensure the Church's rights to the castle a curse was invoked on anyone who should wrest it from the bishopric in the future. This holy curse seems to have been effective after Sherborne ceased to be Church property — some of its unlucky owners included the Earl of Somerset and Sir Walter Raleigh who were both executed.

The ghost of Sir Walter Raleigh haunts Sherborne's grounds, appearing on St Michael's Eve, close to a tree which is named after him.

*Chapter 12*

# Pipes and Drums

High on the wall of Duntrune Castle the piper gazed over the Sound of Jura, and out of the haze he saw a boat take shape which he recognised as belonging to his master. He took a deep breath and began playing a special 'pibroch' which he prayed would make the vessel turn back. As the wild notes carried their message of warning over the water the piper was suddenly seized and dragged away.

'So you tried to trick us,' said the leader of the Campbell clansmen. 'For that you must be taught a lesson — a lesson which will put an end to your tunes.'

Warriors held the piper so he was powerless to move, his hands were spread out on a table and a claymore rose and fell, severing his fingers. But if the Campbells thought that would be the end of his piping they were wrong. Down the centuries the skirl of his phantom bagpipes has echoed over the castle.

The story of the Phantom Piper of Duntrune goes back to 1615 when feuding between the Campbells and Macdonalds was at its height. At this time Coll Ciotach, of the Macdonald clan, had captured Duntrune Castle and garrisoned it with his followers, after which he sailed south to the Isle of Islay.

While he was away the Campbells of Duntrune, who had been masters of the castle for five centuries, counterattacked and retook the fortress, killing every Macdonald except Coll Ciotach's piper. In those days pipers — because of their musical skill — were regarded, like heralds, as privileged persons.

The piper knew that when his master returned he would run straight into an ambush at the castle — somehow he must find a way of warning him that Duntrune was back in the hands of his enemies. In a flash of inspiration he decided to compose a special piece of bagpipe music — a pibroch — which to this day is known as 'The Piper's Warning to his Master'.

From then on he remained at the highest point of the castle, his eyes roving anxiously over the water in the hope of being the first to pick out the Macdonald boat. At last he saw it and he began to play.

The eerie tune floated over the sound, and in his galley Coll Ciotach realised that this was no ordinary welcome. There was something wild and urgent about the melody . . . something that hinted of danger. He ordered his sailors to heave to while he squinted at the castle and the piper silhouetted against the sky.

Apart from that tiny figure Duntrune seemed deserted. Where were his clansmen who should have been coming down to the shore to greet their leader? The more Coll puzzled about it, and the more he listened to the sad wail of the pipes, the more suspicious he became. He shouted a command to his helmsman, and the vessel turned and sped away.

At the castle the Campbells, realising the loyal piper had robbed them of their prey, had their revenge, and the piper soon died from loss of blood and was buried beneath the flagstones of the castle kitchen. A hundred years ago restoration work was undertaken at Duntrune, and beneath the ancient slabs of the kitchen a skeleton was discovered — with its finger bones missing. It was given a proper burial by the Dean of Argyll.

The sound of a Kennedy piper haunts Culzean Castle

which today is a collection of Georgian buildings surrounding an ancient tower which was once the stronghold of the Kennedy clan. In the sixteenth century the family divided, and in 1601 the two sides actually fought a battle, the Kennedys of Culzean becoming the victors. Whether the phantom piper goes back to this time I do not know, but it is not unusual, when the cold wind howls from the Firth of Clyde, for the lament of his pipes to be heard above the gale.

*Rat-tat-tat! Rat-tat-tat!*

Margaret Dalrymple drew back the curtain and looked out to see who was beating a drum beneath her window, but the dusk which had fallen on the Tayside castle of Cortachy was too thick for her to make out anything.

*Rat-tat-tat! Rat-tat-tat!*

Odd, she thought as she continued to dress for dinner. It was her first visit to the castle and she wondered if it was some sort of tradition which the earl liked to keep up, perhaps a ceremonial way of summoning the guests to the dining hall.

A moment later the unseen drummer ceased his tattoo and soon afterwards Margaret's maid, Mrs Ann Day, came into the room.

'Have you any idea why someone should beat a drum down in the courtyard, Ann?' Margaret asked.

'No, miss. I certainly didn't hear anything.'

During dinner Margaret's curiosity got the better of her and turning to her host Lord Airlie, she asked, 'My lord, who is your drummer?'

At this question the earl turned pale, while his wife and several members of the dinner party looked embarrassed. Realising that she had unknowingly said something out of place, she hurriedly began to talk about something else.

After dinner she had an opportunity to speak alone to a member of the family in the drawing-room. She explained that she had not wished to cause any unpleasantness, and she was mystified as to how the mention of the drummer could have had the effect it did.

'What, have you never heard of the drummer boy!' was the reply.

'No. Who in the world is he?' Margaret asked.

'Why, he is a person who goes about the house playing his drum whenever a death is impending in the family. The last time he was heard was shortly before the death of the last countess — the earl's former wife — and that is why Lord Airlie became so pale when you mentioned it. The drummer is a very unpleasant subject in this family, I assure you!'

Margaret decided to say nothing more about the incident, but the next morning, while she was at breakfast with the family, her maid heard the beating of a drum. At first it sounded as though it was below, in the courtyard, then it seemed to echo in the house, getting louder and louder as though approaching the turret in which she and her mistress were lodged. It sounded outside the door, then stopped.

The following morning Margaret had exactly the same experience as Mrs Day. She was so upset by the phenomenon that she cut short her stay at the castle.

Margaret Dalrymple's experience was written up by Catherine Crowe in her book *The Night Side of Nature*, and she described how Lord Airlie's second wife died soon after the drumming had been heard. 'I have heard that a paper was found in her desk after her death,' she wrote, 'declaring her conviction that the drum was for her. . . .'

But who was the Phantom Drummer of Cortachy Castle? Three different stories behind the ill-omened drumming have been handed down through the centuries. The first was that a drummer boy was taken prisoner in a clan feud with the Campbells and was held at Airlie Castle in Angus — then the home of the family — during the reign of Charles I. The unlucky captive perished when the castle was burnt down in 1641 and his vengeful spectre followed James Ogilvy, the first Earl of Airlie, when he moved to nearby Cortachy.

The second story is that the drummer was a herald from the Lindsay clan, who were frequently in conflict with the lords of Airlie, and that the arrogant message he delivered after playing a roll on his instrument so enraged the Earl of Airlie that he had the unfortunate youth seized and hurled from the top of the castle wall.

The most popular account of the tragedy is that the earl believed that a good-looking young drummer in his service was having a love affair with his wife. In a jealous rage he ordered his guards to seize the youth, squeeze him into his own drum and roll it into space from the top of the highest tower.

The drummer was not killed instantly. When the earl went to the foot of the castle wall to see the result of his cruel order, the victim managed to gasp out a curse before he died — swearing that his ghost would haunt the earl's descendants as long as they held the castle. To make matters worse for the earl he soon discovered that his jealousy had been mistaken — the drummer was really his wife's brother, whose identity she had kept secret because he had been outlawed.

In Cortachy Castle today there are the remains of an ancient drum which legend says was played by the drummer.

A giant phantom nearly three metres tall is believed to patrol the battlemented walls of Herstmonceux Castle from time to time, his drumsticks beating out the same tattoo which once rolled over the battlefield of Agincourt — which makes him one of our senior ghosts as the battle took place on St Crispin's Day (25 October) in 1415. Such a magnificient spectre is in keeping with this grand East Sussex castle which has such a vast moat it looks as though it rises out of a lake and is a perfect subject for a storybook illustration, with graceful

98

towers and turrets and a many-arched bridge joining it to the land.

Since 1948 it has housed the Royal Greenwich Observatory, the city air above the original observatory having become too polluted for star-gazing. The present castle was built by Sir Roger de Fiennes who took his drummer with him when he went to fight with Henry V at Agincourt. The man was among the six score of Henry's troops who were killed in that remarkable three-hour battle in which English archers slew more of the enemy than their own force of eight thousand. His loyalty to his master was so strong that his shade returned to Herstmonceux to re-enact the drumming which signalled the archers to release their deadly showers of arrows.

A more matter-of-fact explanation for the drumming was once put forward, suggesting that it was the work of a gardener employed at the castle to keep members of the family out of the way while smugglers carried contraband to be hidden in the castle vaults. This theory is given weight by the fact that there is a room in the castle known as Drummer's Hall which was used by a French gardener, but to me it seems unlikely that the owners of Herstmonceux could have been fooled so easily. It is possible that drumming might have been used to keep away superstitious villagers while smuggling went on, but it would only have been effective if a Phantom Drummer was already feared. Another point is that the Phantom Drummer is a very old tradition of the castle, spanning a much longer period than one man's lifetime.

There is an even stranger story, suggesting that the drumbeats were made by a living person. When a certain elderly Lord Dacre was the owner of the castle he became so religious that he decided to model his life on the early Christian hermits who hid themselves away from the temptations of the world. To do this he retired to a small cell in the castle where he lived on bread and water, and allowed the outside world to think he was dead.

In order to keep visitors from seeing his young and beautiful wife, His Lordship beat a drum at night on the castle ramparts in the hope that their dread of the drummer would keep them away. Lady Dacre had no wish to lead a hermit's life like her old husband, so she locked the door of the recluse's cell and left him to starve to death. But the Phantom Drummer continued to beat his drum long after Lord Dacre had turned to dust in his hidden retreat.

Apart from the drummer, Herstmonceux Castle has other phantoms. In 1727, when part of the castle was in a ruinous condition, an heiress was also starved to death. To prevent her inheriting her rightful property her governess was bribed to lure her to a remote chamber and imprison her. The girl died of hunger on the eve of her twenty-first birthday, and since then her shade has been seen at the edge of the broad moat.

Augustus Hare wrote about the ghost of a sleep-walker, who perhaps fell to his death from the ramparts, and who also haunts Herstmonceux and slowly fades away when seen. Yet another phantom is that of a man with a pigtail dressed in old-fashioned sailor's clothes.

The midnight appearance of four spectral huntsmen galloping in the vicinity of the estate goes back to 1541 when wild Lord Dacre, who was master of the castle at that time, suggested an unusual hunt to his companions, George Roydon, John Frowdys and John Mantell. He had fallen out with a neighbour named Sir Nicholas Pelham, and he thought it would be a great joke to hunt his deer by moonlight. When the moon was high enough, the reckless quartet galloped over the castle drawbridge and across the fields to the Pelham estate. Close to the Cuckmere river they encountered a game-keeper with two companions who angrily ordered them off. When the trespassers greeted his words with laughter he went for them with his staff.

Lord Dacre and his friends unsheathed their swords — perhaps playfully at first — and the sound of steel striking

100

hard wood rang through the trees. Suddenly the game-keeper fell, with blood spurting from a sword wound.

The hunters galloped off, and the dying gamekeeper was carried home where he told Sir Nicholas he had recognised his assailants as Lord Dacre and his friends.

The other two men backed up his story, and when the victim died a couple of days later Lord Dacre and his friends were charged with murder. Because he was a noble he was housed in the Tower of London and tried by his peers, but like Roydon, Frowdys and Mantell he was found guilty and sentenced to death.

There was a lot of argument over the verdict, many people believing that the young lord was guilty of man-slaughter rather than murder as the gamekeeper's death had been the result of a fight in the darkness and there had been no intent to kill him.

Just before the execution it seemed that Henry VIII would grant Lord Dacre a reprieve, and a sixteenth-century historian wrote: 'On the 18th of June the sheriffs of London were ready at the Tower to receive the prisoner and lead him to execution on Tower Hill; but a gentleman of the Lord Chancellor's house came and in the King's name ordered a stay of execution until two in the afternoon, which caused many to think that the King would have granted him his pardon.'

But no further word came and Lord Dacre and his friends were executed. Meanwhile, according to tradition, the Phantom Drummer of Herstmonceux had beaten an eerie prelude to their deaths.

From a military point of view, Dover Castle has ranked second only to the Tower of London in British history. Its strategic value has been recognised from pre-Roman times and within its precincts are the twenty-four-metre-high remains of a Roman light-house. In their turn the Normans also recognised the importance of the site and built much of the castle which is to be seen today, surrounding it with two walls, the inner having fourteen towers and the outer twenty.

In 1216 the castle withstood a siege by the army of the French dauphin, who had been invited to England by the barons to depose King John. A less glorious page of its history was written during the Civil War when a dozen supporters of Parliament, led by a merchant from the town, climbed over one of the walls and talked the Royalist castellan into opening his gates. A Roundhead detachment had to make a forced march from Canterbury to secure the merchant's victory.

During the Napoleonic Wars the castle was regarded as a key defence point, and over two hundred cannons were installed there. It was at this time that a drummer boy was murdered within its walls – presumably by having his head cut off, for the spectre which haunts the castle with a drum is headless.

## Chapter 13

# Castles of Mystery

A phantom panther with glowing eyes padding along the passages of St Donat's Castle on the South Glamorgan coast was just one aspect of a mysterious outbreak of ghostly activity which occurred there at the beginning of the century. No explanation was ever found for the panther or any other of the terrifying supernatural occurrences, which included a mysterious light which glowed in one of the bedrooms like 'a large, glaring eye', a witchlike wraith glimpsed in the armoury, and an invisible pianist who produced chords from a piano even when the lid was locked in place.

Such was the fear caused by these manifestations that the owner decided to sell the property. He advertised it in *Country Life*, but before he received any replies he heard of an exorcist experienced in dealing with such matters and wrote asking him for help.

When the exorcist arrived at St Donat's he listened to a recital of the hauntings and then, having asked the owner to sit in the hall with the main door wide open, retired to the room where the strange eyelike light glowed. Here he prayed and concentrated on dispelling the restless spirits until suddenly a great gust of wind swirled about him, then blew down the staircase and through the hall, practically toppling the owner, and out of the open doorway.

The present baronial hall was constructed in the sixteenth century on the site of a castle built a couple of centuries earlier by Guillaume le Esterling, an ancestor of the Stradling family who held the estate until the middle of the eighteenth century.

According to legend a Lady Stradling was done to death by a member of the family and since then her ghost has been seen from time to time at St Donat's. She has been described as a beautiful ghost who appeared when any mishap was about to befall a member of the house of Stradling. She wore high-heeled shoes and a long trailing gown of finest silk, and the howling of all the dogs in the neighbourhood announced the materialisation of her spectre, which walked either in the castle or its grounds.

As though this family ghost were not enough, the Stradlings were also haunted by a Gwrach-y-rhibyn. This haglike apparition appeared before the death of a member of the family, and there are reports of its having been seen and heard at St Donat's.

Prior to the death of the last Stradling in direct descent, a guest at the castle was aroused in the dead of night by an eerie wail echoing outside his window. He said it sounded like a woman in acute distress, and this was followed by frenzied scratching at the panes of glass.

He told himself that it could be an effect of the wind, that it was not long fingernails scraping the window but most likely a branch. Nevertheless he kept his light burning, and in the morning asked his hostess if she had heard the eerie noise. She answered that she had heard it, and on other occasions too — it was the Gwrach-y-rhibyn which for generations had been a harbinger of death to her family, she declared. To bear out her words news came soon afterwards that the head of the family had died.

The mysterious appearance and disappearance of a cowled figure at Jedburgh Castle in Borders Regions is said to have inspired the great horror writer Edgar Allan Poe's masterpiece *The Masque of the Red Death.*

The castle you see today was opened as a prison in 1832, but the original building was constructed in the twelfth century and became a royal residence for Scotland's kings. It was there· in October 1285 that Alexander III was married to Jolande, the daughter of the Count of Dreux. It was an important marriage both for the king and for Scotland. Alexander had been married before but he was still without an heir, and he knew that unless he married again and had a son, Scotland would be doomed to a bitter power struggle when he died. Therefore, there was great hope in his heart when he stood beside his beautiful bride in the midst of the festivities after the service had been completed. Wine flowed, servants staggered beneath the weight of spitted beasts, jugglers performed extraordinary tricks and the music of minstrels filled the hall.

Suddenly there was a break in the chatter, the music of the harp faded away, an acrobat remained poised in the middle of his routine, and all eyes slowly turned to a tall cowled figure which had appeared without announcement. The menace of the silent intruder immediately killed the fun of the feast. Although Poe's story was pure fiction, his words give an idea of what the Jedburgh apparition must have looked like.

'The figure was tall and gaunt,' he wrote, 'and shrouded from head to foot in the habiliments of the grave. The mask which concealed the visage was made as nearly to resemble the countenance of a stiffened corpse that the closest scrutiny must have had difficulty in detecting the cheat. . . .'

To return to King Alexander's wedding feast — the strange apparition which caused such consternation suddenly vanished as mysteriously as it had come.

It was regarded as a portent of death, and Thomas the Rhymer predicted that it foretold a troubled time for Scotland, beginning on 16 March. He was right, for that very day Alexander died without having fathered a son to inherit his crown. But who – or what – was the figure which appeared so briefly at his wedding?

Melgund Castle, near Brechin, has an even more eerie legend connected with a feast. The owners of the castle invited the neighbouring gentry to celebrate some important family event. When the guests arrived they found the castle brilliantly illuminated with torch and candlelight. In the banqueting hall the tables were laid and the wine was ready to be poured, but there was no one to greet them. The host and his family had vanished and their fate was never known.

The mystery of Dunraven Castle, whose ruins in Mid-Glamorgan overlook the Bristol Channel, is why it is haunted by a Green Lady. With its crumbling walls and little tower surrounded by white skeletal trees, it looks exactly the sort of place which should be haunted by a Green Lady, but in such cases there is usually a clue to her identity. Here she is unknown.

The castle is not the easiest to find. To reach it I followed the B4265 to Southerndown, which overlooks a delightful bay of light-coloured sand and shelves of rock full of fascinating pools. From here I had to take a path up a hill and through some woods to find the remains. The peaceful ivy-covered masonry gives little idea of how the castle must have looked when Francis Grosse, the author of *The Antiquities of England and Wales*, wrote of it in 1773:

Dunraven Castle is built on a high rocky headland, running out a considerable distance into the sea, and forming a point called by the natives, the Witches' Point. The Vaughans, it is said, held it for some time; and according to tradition, the last proprietor of that family used to set up lights, along the shore, and made use of other devices to mislead seamen, in order that they might be wrecked on his manor. This wicked practice, as the popular story goes, did not escape its punishment in this world, three of his sons being drowned in one day. . . .

Was the Green Lady one of the victims of the wreckers? Or was she the mother of the drowned boys whose spirit remained earthbound on account of her grief?

The accident, which some say was supernatural revenge on the Vaughans, occurred within sight of the castle. Not far from the shore is a large rock called the Swifcar which is only visible at low tide. One day two of the wrecker's sons rowed out to the rock to amuse themselves, but in landing they did not moor their boat properly.

'On the rising of the tide it was carried away,' wrote Mr Grosse, 'and they left to all the horrors of their fate, which was inevitable, as the family had no other boat, nor was there any one in the neighbourhood. Their distress was descried from the house, which was filled with confusion and sorrow, in so much that an infant who was just able to walk, being left alone, fell into a vessel of whey, and was drowned almost at the same instant as his two brothers. . . .'

There is another story connected with the Vaughans and their horrible trade of luring ships on to the rocks. One night, after the head of the family had organised a wrecking by hanging lanterns on the horns of cattle and letting them wander along the shore to confuse the sailors, one of his men came to the castle with a ghastly trophy. It was the severed hand of the drowned captain, and on one of the fingers was an unusual ring.

Instead of being delighted when his grinning henchman showed it to him, the normally cold-blooded Vaughan turned white and collapsed. He had recognised the ring as belonging to his own son.

The ghost of a gentleman which has appeared at

107

Greystoke Castle near Penrith in Cumbria has never given a clue to the mystery of his disappearance when he was a living guest at the castle. The castle was originally a Border pele or defence tower, built in 1353 by Lord Greystoke, but has been added to so that it looks rather like an Elizabethan house. It is to the original tower that the mysterious spectre returns.

When Charles Howard, Duke of Norfolk, was master of Greystoke he invited a friend to stay at the castle and hunt with him. After a day in the field and a jolly supper, the guest retired to his room in the old pele tower.

The next morning he did not come down to breakfast, and when he had not appeared by midday, his host sent a servant to rouse him so he would be dressed in time for lunch. The man returned with a puzzled expression and reported that the guest was not in his room, yet he could not have left the castle because his clothes were still folded over the back of a chair.

The staff of the castle were ordered to search the whole building and the grounds around it, but no clue was found as to the riddle of the vanishing guest. And to this day it remains unsolved. The room was not used from then on — and quite understandably because not only has the phantom of the missing guest been glimpsed there, but there is an even more sinister supernatural echo, or echoes, from the past. This is a loud knocking which comes from one of the walls as though someone or something were trying to break through. It is said to be the noise made by a monk who was imprisoned — some say walled up — in an underground passage which once led from the tower to a chapel in the grounds of the castle.

A man who returned to watch his own funeral is the mystery associated with Scotney Castle in Kent. Although small, it is one of the most beautiful castles in England, especially when you see its reflection among the waterlilies of the moat. To be found in the middle of vast, slightly wild gardens, it was built in the fourteenth century by Roger Ashburnham. Later it passed into the hands of the Catholic Darrell family.

The riddle connected with Scotney was posed on 12 December 1720 at the funeral of Arthur Darrell who had died while on the Continent. When the coffin was lowered into the grave the mourners noticed in their midst a stranger muffled in a black cloak, and as the clods began to thud on the coffin lid the unknown man remarked: 'That is me they think they are burying!'

After this remark he vanished. According to some accounts, he disappeared before their eyes.

Was it the ghost of Arthur Darrell, or did he have some secret reason for wishing to be thought to be dead?

John Bailey, a sexton who died in 1867, claimed that when he was preparing a grave in the Scotney Chapel of Lamberhurst Church he came upon an iron studded coffin unexpectedly and, prising off the lid to try and find out who it contained, saw it to be full of stones. We cannot be certain that this was Arthur's coffin, and if it was, why did he risk detection by attending his own funeral? The mystery of Scotney remains.

Another castle with a mysterious interment is Dunster which sits protectively above the Somerset village of that name. The thatched cottages, washed pink or white, look almost too much like a tourist poster to be true – to walk between them gives you a feeling of having accidentally wandered on to some historical film set. The castle, which dates from Norman times and was held on behalf of the Empress Matilda by William de Mohun against the forces of King Stephen, must once have been the scene of some dark deed, for when work was being carried out on the gatehouse a *chained* skeleton was found. It was that of a man nearly two metres tall, whose neck, ankles and wrists were secured by fetters.

It is believed his burial might have dated back to when the castle was being besieged by King Stephen's troops, but even if he was an enemy prisoner why should he have been bound with links of iron? Economy would surely have made his captors remove the chains once he was dead — or were the shackles left purposely to restrain him after death?

It was the 'horrid sound of knocking' during a funeral which heralded the haunting of Lowther Castle which today stands like a great turreted shell with wild Border sky showing through its blind windows.

It was built in the seventeenth century, damaged by fire in 1720 and restored nearly a century later, only to fall into romantic decay again. Its owners, the Lowther family, were said to have settled in the area generations before William the Conqueror came to England, their name being derived from the Danish words 'louth' and 'er' which signify 'fortune' and 'honour'. The apparition which haunted Lowther Castle goes back to the extra-ordinary Sir James Lowther, who became the first Lord Lonsdale in 1784.

Thomas De Quincey, famous for his *Confessions of an English Opium-Eater*, and who lived for some time in the Lake District, wrote of him:

> He was a true Feudal chieftain. The coach in which he used to visit Penrith was old and neglected; his horses fine and untrimmed, and such was the impression diffused about him by his gloomy temper and habits of oppression that, according to the declaration of a Penrith contemporary of the old despot, the streets were silent as he traversed them, and an awe sat upon many faces. . . . Superstition made his 'ghost' more terrible and notorious after his death than the verit-able 'despot' had been during his life.

This eccentric noble, who surrounded his castle with herds of wild horses, fell desperately in love with a young woman who, by the standards of those days, was 'not his social equal'. This meant nothing to him and he persuaded her to live with him. Leaving his residence to the wild horses, he set up home in a great Hampshire house where a whole army of servants was engaged to serve the lady.

Despite the beautiful home, the servants and the riches, the girl did not find the happiness she expected — perhaps she was overawed by his rank and wealth.

The last act of the tragedy for Sir James came when his beloved mistress was taken ill and died. His grief was so terrible that none of the servants dared mention the fact that death had claimed her. The earl left her body on her bed, and such was his domineering character and obsession that even the butler, as the head of the servants, was too terrified to suggest that the corpse be given proper burial.

Finally the smell of decomposition became so revolting the servants decided that unless Sir James could be persuaded to have the body buried they must leave. It fell to the lot of the valet to speak to his lordship, but no sooner had he mentioned the subject than Sir James drove him from the room with curses and ordered him never to speak to him again.

At last sanity must have returned to Sir James for he made arrangements for the body to be buried at a cemetery in Paddington. But even this was no straight-forward operation. The eccentric earl ordered a detach-ment of the Cumberland militia to be sent down to London to mount guard night and day at the cemetery until the tomb was finished.

After the funeral had finally taken place the earl wore deep mourning for his mistress for the rest of his life.

With such a strange character it was almost to be expected that his spirit would be restless and would return to haunt Lowther Castle.

The manifestations began at his own funeral. During the service came a sound of knocking. Then as the pallbearers lifted the coffin it seemed possessed of some strange power which made it sway so alarmingly that

111

only with great difficulty did the men manage to carry it to the graveside. A certain Mr Sullivan, who had a local reputation for 'keeping records', and who was present at the grotesque ceremony, wrote: 'He was with difficulty buried, and whilst the clergyman was praying over him, he very nearly knocked the reverend gentleman from his desk! When placed in the grave, the power of creating alarm was not interred with his bones. There were disturbances in the hall, noises in the stables; neither men nor animals were suffered to rest. . . .'

The ghostly earl was not only responsible for poltergeist phenomena within Lowther Castle. At night his coach and six – which had caused such awe in the streets of Penrith – was seen hurtling along the roads near to the castle. Although the spectral carriage was often heard and observed, and the earl made his presence felt through continual disturbances in the castle, his phantom never made a visible appearance.

At last the supernatural activity became too much for the inhabitants of the castle and the local people asked a priest to exorcise the restless earl, which he did.

A haunting without a known explanation takes place at the great Roman fort known as Burgh whose massive flint-faced walls were raised in the third century to protect the 'Saxon Shore'. Located at the meeting of the Yare and Waveney rivers, nearly five kilometres southwest of Great Yarmouth, it is an awe-inspiring monument to the Roman military engineers. Tradition has it that annually on 3 July a corpse wrapped in a white banner is thrown by unseen hands from the top of one of its five-metre-high ramparts, only to vanish the moment it strikes the ground.

## Chapter 14

# The Victims' Return

Through the dusk Christmas trees glittered behind the village windows as a visitor walked along the main street of Bramber in West Sussex. It was a chilly Christmas Eve, the only sign of life was the lines of smoke rising from the chimneys, and he was surprised when he saw two small forms standing still, gazing up at the ruined tower of Bramber Castle which dominates the village.

What surprised the man was not that he should see two children, but that they should be wearing rags. Then, as he watched in amazement, they turned to him and he saw that their faces were practically skull-like through starvation. It seemed unbelievable that such ragged and hungry children could be found in the England of today. . . .

He moved forward to speak to them, but as he did so they melted away and to his horror he found himself alone beneath the great tower.

Bramber Castle was built towards the end of the eleventh century on a natural mound above the River Adur. One of its early inhabitants was William de Braose, and it is his children who are still to be glimpsed gazing at the ruin of their old home, or running hand in hand through the village.

Their tragedy began when King John took them as hostages, as an old historian described:

In the year 1208, King John suspecting divers of the nobility sent to demand hostages for their fidelity, among the rest to William de Braose of whom his messengers demanded his children which Matilda his wife, according to Matthew Paris, gave this answer, that she could not trust her children with the King, who had so basely murdered his own nephew, Prince Arthur, whom he was in honour bound to protect. This speech being reported to the King, he was greatly insensed thereat and secretly sent soldiers to seize the whole family. But they receiving private information of his intent fled to Ireland, where he, in the year 1210, making them prisoners sent them to England and, closely confining them in Windsor Castle, he caused them to be starved to death. Some say William escaped to France where he shortly after died.

Since then the spectres of the two murdered children have returned to Bramber where they had enjoyed brief happiness before the messengers of the king arrived. If you should ever see them as evening is drawing on they will hold out their thin hands as though begging for food but − like the Gilsland Boy − they will fade away the moment you speak to them.

Many different kinds of ghosts haunt British castles. Some reappear from time to time always in the same place and doing the same thing, rather as though they are images on a piece of cinema film being played over and over again. Other phantoms seem to have wills of their own, materialising in a castle dungeon at one time and perhaps on its ramparts the next, and sometimes acting as though they have some message they want to convey to the living. It was such a ghost which once returned from the grave to bring her murderer to justice.

This happened at Cawood Castle, today a privately owned property in North Yorkshire, but originally the palace of the Archbishop of York and built on the site of

King Athelstan's hall. It was fortified during the reign of Henry IV, and its surviving gatehouse is now incorporated into a farm building.

The drama began on 14 April, 1690, when William Barwick went walking with his wife Mary under the walls of the castle. The couple did not get on well together, they frequently quarrelled and his feelings for her had turned to resentment. On a savage impulse he suddenly seized her and pushed her into a pond, holding her beneath the surface of the stagnant water until the bubbles ceased to rise. Then he waded out, dragging the body of his victim to the edge of the pond where he hid it among the bulrushes.

The next night he went back to the castle and in the moonlight took a hay spade from a nearby rick, dug a shallow grave on the bank and buried his wife. Barwick then went to the house of his brother-in-law, Thomas Lofthouse, and told him that Mary had gone to her uncle's house in Selby.

A description of what followed was given in John Aubrey's *Miscellanies*, published in the last century:

But Heaven would not be so deluded, but raised up the ghost of the murdered woman to make the discovery. And therefore it was upon the Easter Tuesday following, about two of the clock in the afternoon, the forementioned Lofthouse having occasion to water a quickset hedge, not far from his house; as he was going for the second pail full, an apparition went before him in the shape of a woman, and soon after sat down upon a rising green grass-plot, right over against the pond; he walked by her as he went to the pond; and as he returned with the pail from the pond, looking sideways to see whether she continued in the same place, he found she did. . . . So soon as he had emptied his pail, he went into his yard, and stood still to try whether he could see her again, but she was vanished.

In this information he says, that the woman seemed to be habited in a brown coloured petticoat, waistcoat, and a white hood; such a one as his wife's sister usually wore, and that her countenance looked extremely pale and wan, with her teeth in sight, but no gums appearing, and that her physiognomy was like to that of his wife's sister, who was wife to William Barwick.

For the rest of the day Lofthouse was worried by what he had seen and, after evening prayers, told his wife that he believed that he had seen a ghost by Cawood Castle. Mrs Lofthouse feared her sister was the victim of foul play and told her husband to search for her as soon as it was daylight. Lofthouse recalled how Barwick had told him about his wife going to her uncle's house and went straight to Selby to see if she really was with him. He learned that no one in that household had seen Mr and Mrs Barwick.

Thomas Lofthouse was now so suspicious of his brother-in-law that he went to the Lord Mayor of York and, explaining his suspicions, had a warrant of arrest made out for him.

On 16 September of that year William Barwick pleaded not guilty before Sir John Powel at the York assizes. At first he denied a confession he had made earlier and explained he had sold his wife for five shillings − a custom not so uncommon in those days − but he was not able to give any details or name the man who had taken her.

The confession was then read:

*The examination of William Barwick, taken the twenty-fifth day of April, 1690.*

WHO sayeth and confesseth, that he carried his wife over a certain wain-bridge, called Bishopdike-bridge, betwixt Cawood and Sherborne, and within a lane about one hundred yards from the said bridge, and on the left hand of the said bridge, he and he wife went over a stile, on the left hand of a certain gate, entering into a certain close on the left hand of the said lane; and in a pond in the said close, adjoining to a quick-wood-hedge, did drown his wife, and upon the bank of the said pond, did bury her; and further, that he was within sight of Cawood Castle, on the left hand; and that there was but one hedge betwixt the said close, where he drowned his said wife, and the Bishopslates belonging to the said castle.

After Thomas Lofthouse had given his evidence – in which he described how he had seen the ghost – and the court had heard how the victim's body had been found beside the pond in clothing like that Lofthouse had seen on the apparition, William Barwick was sentenced to death. He was duly executed and his body was left hanging in chains as a dreadful warning.

For nine centuries the phantom of another young woman who had been murdered by her husband is said to have haunted the site of Skipsea Castle in Humberside. Today all that remains of the castle is a gloomy mound surrounded by muddy fields on the east coast between Bridlington and Hornsea, a sombre setting for the ghost known as the White Lady of Skipsea.

At the time of the Norman Conquest she was married to Drogo de Brevere, a Fleming who had enlisted in the mercenary forces recruited by William the Conqueror. For his valour at the Battle of Hastings, Drogo was given the seigniory of the district of Holderness. He made his home in Skipsea Castle which he constructed on a high motte mainly as a defence against the marauding Danes who frequently landed at Flamborough to raid the countryside.

The Saxons and the Danish settlers of Holderness soon learned to detest their new master who confiscated their property and reduced them to serfdom. As well as being an arrogant tyrant, he was more than usually greedy and even tried to seize Church lands, though later he was forced to make restoration by the bishops.

If he was loathed by the peasants, he was still the sort of man that King William needed to 'pacify' his conquered territory, and as a mark of royal approval he arranged a marriage between one of his nieces and Drogo. The girl is thought to have been a granddaughter of Arlette — William's mother — by a second marriage. After the wedding Drogo took his bride to Skipsea Castle, but it was soon clear that the match was an unhappy one — she was a refined Norman lady while he had only the harsh bravery of a soldier of fortune to recommend him, his interests being in hunting, drinking and making life hell for his serfs. And soon he was treating her as badly as any of them. When he was drunk he would threaten to kill her.

At length he put the threat into operation and poisoned her. When he sobered up and saw the body of his wife in the unforgiving light of morning, he realised that when the news reached the girl's royal uncle he would not only lose his estates but his life. For a while he brooded, trying to think of a solution to his criminal folly, then he ran to the stables and, mounting his fastest horse, spurred towards London. Here he went before William, most probably in the White Tower, the oldest part of the Tower of London, and told him that he would like the king's permission to take his wife to Flanders so that he could introduce her to his family.

William agreed, giving Drogo permission to leave as soon as he wished. Drogo then told William that the estate he had at Holderness was so infertile that nothing would grow except oats, and that much of it was only worthless marsh and forest. Then, with a smile of candour, he admitted that he did not have enough cash for the journey. The king ordered his Treasurer to give Drogo a large sum of money, knowing that he needed to keep his barons content if he wished for their continuing support.

As soon as he left court, Drogo took passage on a ship to Flanders. It had only just hoisted its sail when news arrived from Skipsea Castle of the death of William's niece by poisoning. The king immediately sent a party of knights after Drogo but when they reached the port he had gone with the tide. He was soon in Flanders, after which history loses sight of him, but the ghost of his wife has continued to haunt the castle.

Last century the *Hull Advertiser* carried this first-hand account by a gentleman who had seen her:

> I was travelling on horseback one afternoon from Bridlington to Hornsea, and I was descending the brow of a hill, south of Skipsea, when I observed a woman apparently young, dressed in white, walking a little before me on my left hand, between the hedge and the road. Supposing that she had been visiting at a house on the top of a hill, I turned my head to see if there were any persons in attendance at the door, but the door was shut and there were none to be seen.
>
> Curiosity now being greater than before to know who this genteel person was, I followed her at a distance of twenty to thirty yards down the hill which was a hundred or a hundred and fifty yards long, and expected when she got to the bottom, where there was a small brook, to meet her in attempting to gain the carriage bridge.
>
> To my great astonishment, when she approached the brook, instead of turning to the right to gain the bridge, she vanished from my sight, at the very time that my eyes were fixed upon her.
>
> As soon as I got home I related the strange affair to my family; and as it was light and I had not been previously thinking about apparitions, nor was I ever in the habit of ever speculating on such subjects, I am firmly persuaded that what I saw was one.

I found it interesting that of the scores of haunted castles I visited to gather material for this book, hardly any referred to ghosts in their guidebooks. There would be pages of architectural description but no mention of anything supernatural, and I began to wonder if there is something about a ghost which is considered to lower the tone of a castle. A welcome exception to this was magnificent Warwick Castle where not only is the ghost of Sir Fulke Greville described in its literature, but a taped version of the story plays at intervals in the haunted room.

Sir Fulke Greville, first Baron Brooke, was an Elizabethan poet who wrote over a hundred sonnets and a couple of tragedies, and who also served as a Privy Councillor.

While in London in 1628 he was mysteriously stabbed by an old and trusted servant named Ralph Heywood who committed suicide afterwards. Sir Fulke lingered a month before death overtook him. Then his restless spirit returned to his castle which in life he had restored at great expense to 'the most princely seat within the midland parts of this realm' – which is still a good description of Warwick.

The haunted room is Sir Fulke's study in one of the towers and it is furnished just as it would have been when he sat there, quill in hand, before his parchment. Recently Mrs Joan Ryan heard an eerie sound above the noise of her vacuum cleaner when she was working in the room. She described it as a loud 'raking sound' coming from the panelling on which hung a portrait of the murdered gentleman.

'I turned off the machine, and a few moments later I heard the same noise again,' she said. 'I was so frightened I could not even find the key to let myself out of the room. I had never believed in ghosts, but I do now.' After this she refused to work in the tower.

While I was visiting Warwick Castle a lady at the sales counter told me that the ghost of Sir Fulke had been seen in the castle shortly before my arrival.

I came across another odd story of Warwick Castle, written by J. Harvey Bloom in 1918:

An ancient dame had the privilege of selling spare milk [at the castle] and by a system not uncommon to modern milk vendors she so cheated her customers that the earl hearing of it cancelled the privilege. She then bewitched the castle, usually in the form of a black dog. The chaplain and the vicars of St Mary's and St Nicholas brought the evil one to rest by reading passages of scripture, and eventually followed the witch in the form of a dog to the height of Caesar's Tower from which she or it sprang into the stream to a chamber prepared under the milldam. Her statue was placed above the tower battlements until blown down some years back.

Warwick Castle is well worth visiting because it has everything a castle should have — from a defensive mound built by Ethelfleda, daughter of King Alfred, to a magnificent collection of armour in the Great Hall. There is also a display of torture intruments, some of which are from the Nuremberg Castle collection, in the dungeon.

There is a joke that there is only one thing worse than finding a worm in an apple you are eating and that is to find half a worm — and perhaps the same applies to a ghost. A phantom which only appears from the waist up returned to haunt privately-owned Meggernie Castle which is situated halfway up Scotland's longest glen, Glen Lyon. It was here that Captain Robert Campbell and his followers stayed for the night when on their way to Glen Coe to massacre over forty members of the Macdonald clan for their Jacobite sympathies in 1692.

The most vivid account of the Meggernie apparition was written in 1862 by a Mr E. J. Simons, of Westhorpe, after he had been a guest at the castle for a house party. Here he met an old friend by the name of Beaumont Fetherstone, and was delighted when he found that their rooms were adjoining. The rooms were situated in the

121

castle tower, giving them a splendid view of the River Lyon. Simons saw a door in his wall and wondered if it led into his friend's room, but when he tried to open it he found that it was sealed.

He shouted through the keyhole, 'Does this blocked-up door lead into your room?'

Fetherstone shouted back that it did — and it didn't. 'It actually leads into a small closet,' he explained. 'But it's screwed up on my side.'

The friends then visited each other's rooms to examine the door, but when they were unable to open it they went to bed.

Sometime after midnight Simons was awakened by what seemed like a feverish kiss on his cheek, so hot in fact that it made him wince. He jumped out of bed and then to his horror beheld the upper half of a woman gliding towards the sealed door, through which she disappeared.

After a moment he summoned up enough courage to follow her, but when he reached the connecting door he found it fastened as firmly as when he and his friend had examined it. Next he went to a mirror, expecting to see a burn on his face, but — despite the fact that he could still feel the unearthly imprint — there was not a mark to be seen.

Early next morning he sought his friend and told him, 'I've had a most terrible night.'

Fetherstone answered that he had too, but before they described it to each other they must get a third party to hear their stories dispassionately and compare them. They went to their host and gave him almost identical accounts. The result was that both were moved from the tower.

Beaumont Fetherstone was so impressed by his ordeal that he wrote a description of it, part of which read:

At Meggernie Castle, Perthshire, 2 a.m., I was wakened by a pink light in the room, and saw a female at the foot of the bed. At first I took her for a housekeeper walking in her sleep. She came along the side of the bed and bent over me. I raised myself, and she retreated and went into a small room made out of the thickness of the wall, opposite the foot of the bed.

He went on to explain that this closet had no window or fireplace. Though he searched it and his room thoroughly he could find no sign of the mysterious intruder.

'The phantom seemed *minus* legs,' he concluded. 'Which I am glad to say I didn't realise at the first glimpse or I should have been in an even greater funk than I was.'

The explanation for the appearance of the mutilated spectre goes back to when one of the chiefs of the Menzies clan resided there. By nature he was a man who found it difficult to control his almost insane jealousy. One day it reached such a pitch that he murdered his young wife high in the castle tower. When he returned to his senses he began to plan how he could escape retribution. His first act was to cut the corpse in two so he could hide it in a chest standing in the closet which was built into the wall of the chamber.

He then made it known that he and his wife had decided to travel abroad and departed during the night without the servants seeing him off.

Some months later he returned to Meggernie and announced that his wife had been drowned while on holiday. After having expressed gratitude for the sympathy of the staff, who had been very fond of their mistress, he retired to the tower where he unsealed the closet with its hideous secret. When the rest of the castle were asleep, he took the lower half of the corpse from the chest and carried it down the tower stairs and out to a nearby churchyard where he buried it.

It seems the next night he was going to bury the rest of the body – instead it was his body that was found in the tower! He had been murdered by an unknown assailant, most likely some person who had guessed the true cause of the lady's disappearance and avenged her.

## Chapter 15

# Guardians of Treasure

The occupant of the magnificent bedroom looked up and saw by the soft glow of her candle that she was not alone. In front of her was a well-dressed gentleman whom she thought for a moment was the castle butler. A few moments later he left as silently as he had entered and, suddenly aware that no sound had come from the massive lock on her door, the poor woman realised she had been visited by a ghost — and that she had been the victim of a cruel trick.

This drama took place at Powis Castle — known locally as the Red Castle because of the ruddy shade of its limestone walls — which commands the Severn Valley close to Welshpool. In 1780 rumours swept the town that a woman had seen the castle's famed ghost who was said to have revealed a secret to her. John Hampson, a man held in high regard as a preacher by the Wesleyan Methodists, was so curious about the stories that he interviewed the woman.

She explained to him that she was a spinster in both meanings of the word — she was unmarried, and she had earned her living by spinning. As farmers in the district grew their own flax she went to their farmhouses where she spun it on the spot. On one occasion, when her usual customers had no work for her, she decided to try her luck at the Red Castle.

When she arrived at the gloomy fortress she was told by the steward that the Earl of Powis and his family were away in London and he could not say if a spinner was required. But the steward's wife, a woman who hid a cruel streak behind a pleasant smile, found her some sewing work, saying she could stay at the castle and earn her keep until the earl returned. What surprised and delighted the simple spinner was the luxurious room she was allotted. What she did not know was that it was the castle's haunted room and the steward's wife, encouraged by the rest of the servants, had placed her there to see what would happen!

The servants made up a good fire and left a lighted candle on the table. In one corner was a great four-poster bed so comfortable that the spinner could hardly believe such luxury existed. After the servants bade her goodnight she may have wondered why the lock on her door was turned, but perhaps she thought this was the usual practice in great castles, a safeguard so strangers like her would not be tempted to help themselves to the family silver.

Having examined the room, she sat down at the table and in the candlelight read her Bible. Like so many religious-minded people of her time, it was her practice to read a chapter before going to sleep.

After a while she looked up and saw that a man had entered, wearing what she described as a 'gold-lace suit and hat'. She was rather surprised, but again everything was so new to her that at first she was not afraid, thinking that perhaps he was the butler who had come to make sure everything was all right.

The figure walked across the room to a corner window, then turned and stood sideways to her, giving the impression that he expected her to say something. The woman was tongue-tied, but after a little time – during which she tried vainly to think of something to say to the impressive visitor – he walked off, closing the door behind him as the servants had done.

The fact that this time there was no sound of a lock grating suddenly made her aware that he had entered without the key being turned, and for the first time she understood that he was a phantom.

Everything fell into place. The splendid room, coupled with the unusual attentions of the servants, made her realise that she was there to be haunted. Only one thing occurred to her and that was to pray, so she knelt down by her bedside and joining her hands entreated God to protect her.

While she was doing this the gentleman in the gold-lace suit appeared once more and again it seemed as if he were waiting for her to speak. When she was unable to form any words, he disappeared once again through the locked door. She prayed harder that 'God would strengthen her and not suffer her to be tried beyond what she was able to bear'. Perhaps because of her simple faith she found it possible to speak when the apparition appeared for the third time.

'Pray sir, who are you, and what do you want?'

'Take up the candle and follow me and I shall tell you,' the spectre answered.

She rose from her knees, took the candle from the table and followed him out of the room and along a seemingly endless corridor until they reached the door of another room.

The spectre ushered her in and, stooping down, tore up one of the floorboards, under which appeared a box with an iron handle in the lid. Then he stepped to one side of the room and showed her a crevice in the wall where a key was hidden that would open it.

'This box and key must be taken out and sent to the earl in London. Will you see it done?'

'I will do my best to get it done,' she replied.

'Do — and I will trouble the house no more,' he said, then walked out of the room.

The spinner described how she had stepped towards the door and started shouting. 'The steward and his wife,

126

with other servants, came to me immediately, all cling-ing together, with lights in their hands. . . . I told them the story and showed them the box. The steward dared not meddle with it, but his wife had more courage and, with the help of the other servants, tugged it out and found the key.'

The spinner said that the chest was heavy but she did not see it opened and therefore could not say what was in it. The steward and servants carried it away, and ex-hausted by her experience, and at the same time com-forted by the thought that the phantom had meant her no harm, the woman returned to her four-poster and slept until the cocks crowed in the morning.

The steward sent the box to his master in London with a letter describing the curious way it had been found. By return came a letter ordering the steward to tell the spinner that if she wished she could live in the castle for the rest of her life or, if she wished to remain in her cottage, she would be well provided for. The woman accepted the latter offer, being grateful both to the earl and the ghost. But neither she nor Mr Hampson ever heard an explanation for the apparition or got a hint of what was contained in the hidden chest.

A far less pleasant character than the mysterious gentle-man of Powis guarded the golden treasure of Thirlwall Castle, a Border fortress which was built with stones plundered from the Roman Wall and is now just a number of ruined walls. Should you visit it be careful when you are beneath these walls for – as a notice warns you – pieces of ancient masonry crash down from time to time.

For several centuries the castle was the home of the 'Fierce Thirlwalls', and its legend goes back to the days of Baron John de Thirlwall when, as an added deterrent to the castle's foes, a gigantic stone statue stood guard over its ramparts.

When Baron John returned triumphant from some

distant wars, he was followed by a baggage train of loot, the pride of which was a table cast of solid gold guarded by an ugly dwarf whose dark skin proclaimed that his origin was as exotic as that of the table. The fame of the Golden Table of Thirlwall spread across the Border country, and many raids were made by envious Border lords anxious to seize the treasure for themselves.

It was the Scots who finally stormed the castle's defences and butchered the defenders, but when they battered down the heavy door of the chamber in which the gleaming table was supposed to stand they found that it and its guardian had vanished. For a moment the raiders stared about the empty room, cursing with chagrin. Then one of the party rushed in with the news that, as the last of Baron John's retainers had fought for a few more seconds of life, he had glimpsed the black midget staggering to the castle well under the weight of the fabled table. Here he flung it down the shaft and then, with a malicious sneer on his face, jumped after it.

The Scots raced from the chamber to the well, but when they arrived in the courtyard they found the paving stretched from wall to wall without a break. The genie of the table had magically sealed the well opening, and – it would be nice to think – guards his table to this day in some subterranean cavern far below the castle's foundations.

Like Thirlwall Castle, Blenkinsopp Castle has a ghost connected with its hidden treasure. There is a legend that a tunnel connects the two castles but this is unlikely. Stories of secret passages are widespread on the Border but they usually turn out to be disused mining tunnels.

Blenkinsopp is now a creeper-covered ruin, surrounded by a modern residential caravan park. Its history goes back to the fourteenth century when – like Thirlwall – it was built of stone filched from the Roman Wall. The castle is haunted by two ghosts, a phantom hound which is only seen when the owner of the castle is on the point of death, and a White Lady.

The lady's story goes back to Bryan de Blenkinsopp, who was born with an overwhelming desire for riches. On one occasion he was invited to a wedding feast at the hall of another Border family, and during the feasting his neighbour raised his goblet and cried, 'To Bryan and his lady love.' To the surprise of the guests the young man jumped to his feet and declared: 'Never shall that be till I meet a lady possessed of a chest of gold too heavy for ten men to carry into my castle!'

The guests lowered their cups with the toast undrunk, and Bryan de Blenkinsopp sank back into his chair with the uneasy realisation that the wine had made him make a fool of himself. Soon afterwards he left his castle and 'sought a countrie ayont the ocean tide'.

Some years later he returned with a satisfied expression and a foreign bride whose dowry was in a chest which actually required a dozen men to carry it into the castle. The local boy had made good, and the jokes about his boast at the wedding feast turned suddenly sour. But there was gossip about the new lady of the castle because it was said she was a non-Christian, which would suggest that Bryan had met her while on a Crusade. Her foreign servants, too, must have caused her to be regarded with suspicion.

All went well with the marriage until Bryan's wife heard talk of how her husband had announced he would marry wealth, and she believed that it had been for her dowry rather than herself that he had married her. Hurt by the thought — and determined that he should be hurt too — she waited until he was away hunting and then hid the treasure in a vault at the end of a tunnel beneath the castle, a secret place of which even Bryan was unaware.

When he returned he was aghast to find the treasure gone, but his wife ignored his pleas and rages and refused to tell him where it was hidden. In a fury the lord of Blenkinsopp left the castle once again, perhaps on another Crusade.

Once her emotions had run their course, Lady de Blenkinsopp began to miss Bryan and bitterly regretted her dramatic action which had made him quit his ancestral hall. She took to spending her days by the castle gate, listening for the hoofbeats which would herald her husband's return. But the years went by and no news of him reached Blenkinsopp. Finally she left with her strange servants to seek him, and she too never returned — at least not in human form.

Her white phantom has been seen from time to time gliding about the remains of the castle and, according to local folklore, it will continue to do so until the gold is found and its custody passes from her spectral hands. Apparently children are more sensitive to her presence than adults.

## Chapter 16

# Doomed Lovers

There is a spot close to Goodrich Castle in Hereford and Worcester that has long been shunned by courting couples in case the doom which overtook a pair of lovers there should bring bad luck to them. And it is not just the fear of ill fortune which keeps them away — when the wind moans round the castle's shattered towers it is said that sometimes the death cries of the star-crossed lovers can be heard above it.

The mighty sandstone ruins of the thirteenth-century castle rear up on a hill overlooking the River Wye near Goodrich village south of Ross-on-Wye. Its walls rise majestically from a great mound in the centre of what was once a moat.

When the Civil War broke out Roundhead troops garrisoned the castle for a short time before it passed back into the hands of the Royalists who were soon defending it against the Roundheads again. The leader of the Parliamentary forces, Colonel Birch, made a surprise attack but was beaten back, having only managed to burn some stables. He gave up the siege, but returned in 1646 after King Charles had surrendered. The Goodrich Royalists clung to their lost cause until their water supply was cut. After their surrender the castle was heavily damaged by cannon fire.

The haunting of the castle goes back to the time of

131

Colonel Birch's siege. His niece Alice was in love with a Royalist sympathiser named Clifford, and together they had sought refuge in the castle. When her uncle's first attack failed Alice must have believed that they were safe, but then came the news of the king's surrender to the Scots at Newark in May 1646. It was followed by the return of Colonel Birch with more artillery, including huge mortars capable of throwing cannonballs weighing ninety kilograms into the beleaguered castle.

As time passed and the monotonous bombardment shook the castle, Clifford and Alice realised it would only be a matter of time before the combined effects of artillery and thirst forced the defenders to surrender.

One night, when storm clouds obscured the moon, Clifford saddled his horse and, with Alice beside him, managed to lead it out of the castle. On the other side of the moat they both mounted and spurred through the lines of sleeping Roundheads to plunge down the steep slope which led to the Wye. Here they hoped to cross the ford and make their escape.

But they had not bargained on the heavy rain which had caused the river to flood. A moment after Clifford had urged his reluctant mount into the water they were swept away to their deaths.

On the anniversary of their tragedy a horseman, with a lady mounted behind him, is said to enter the river at the ford and then disappear beneath the dark current.

A girl, her body transfixed by an arrow and with an expression of terror beneath her wildly flowing hair, is the spectre of Rochester Castle who is still seen after seven centuries. The name of the distraught ghost was Lady Blanche de Warrene, and she was betrothed to Ralph de Capo, the lord of Rochester Castle which still dominates the Medway as it has done for almost a thousand years.

The first castle was built on the site of a Roman camp by Bishop Gundulf in the 1080s and the keep is an example of the square stone ones introduced into

132

England by the Normans. It was first besieged by King John in 1215 when over a hundred rebel knights defied him until starvation forced them to surrender.

It was in 1264, when the castle was besieged by Simon de Montfort, that tragedy overtook Lady Blanche — with the result that her restless shade still returns to the ancient battlements.

Ralph de Capo, having proved himself as a valiant warrior in the Crusades, bitterly resisted de Montfort's army.

Serving under de Montfort was Sir Gilbert de Clare who had a particular desire to see the castle fall as he had been rejected by Lady Blanche.

De Montfort's forces were less successful at besieging Rochester than King John's had been, and in the end he raised the siege. As the army was leaving Sir Ralph and his knights sallied forth from the castle to harry the retreating rebels. During the confusion Sir Gilbert de Clare dressed himself in a surcoat which had the same device worked on it as that worn by Sir Ralph. Thus disguised, he rode to the undefended castle and climbed to the battlements where Lady Blanche was watching the distant fighting.

Suddenly she looked round to see Sir Gilbert, and she knew he was thirsting for revenge for the slight she had given him before the siege. She fled along the top of the battlemented wall, which still rises thirty-four metres above the ground, to seek sanctuary in the Round Tower where she barricaded the door and climbed its circular staircase to the top. Sir Gilbert's battleaxe soon smashed the door and Blanche knew her choice lay between being captured by the brutal knight or leaping from the highest castle in the country.

Meanwhile Sir Ralph de Capo was returning at the head of his cavalry, smiling with grim satisfaction at the result of the foray against his enemies. But as he looked up at his castle, he saw two struggling figures silhouetted on top of the Round Tower. Realising his fiancée was being attacked, he leapt to the ground, seized a bow from an archer and fired an arrow. It flew in a great arc to the top of the tower and struck his enemy, but Sir Gilbert's armour deflected the arrow straight into the heart of Lady Blanche. She slumped to the paving stones of the tower with the bitter knowledge that her lover had accidentally brought about her death.

We do not know the fate that overtook Sir Gilbert de Clare, but one can imagine that he paid fully for his crime. And it was recorded that the same night as she died, Lady Blanche's ghost was seen walking the castle walls, weeping at her cruel destiny.

It was also a siege which led to the haunting of Ludlow Castle at the town of the same name west of Kidderminster. During the reign of Henry II there was much bitter fighting in the border area, and frequently the garrison of Ludlow Castle rode out to defend the town against the Welsh raiders. On one such occasion, when the castle was left with only a handful of soldiers guarding it, a girl by the name of Marion de la Bruyère lowered a rope so her lover could keep a tryst with her.

One can imagine her excitement as, looking over the battlements, she saw his figure climbing lithely up to her. Next minute she was in his arms and she was so engrossed she forgot the rope had been left dangling. The young man took care to lead her away from the spot, and for a while she lay happily in his arms.

Suddenly a sound made her glance along and she saw another figure appear over the battlements, followed by another and another – and Marion realised she had been deceived. Almost demented at the realisation of how she had been tricked, she pulled the dagger from her false lover's belt and ran it into his heart. Then she ran to the top of the grimly named Hanging Tower and leapt into space – to die on the rocks far below.

Over a hundred men scaled up Marion's rope, and soon had the castle under their control. But stories began to spread that Marion's white form had been seen re-enacting the drama she had played out on the Hanging Tower — a drama which for centuries has denied her spirit rest.

Another phenomenon which dates back to that tragedy is a strange rasping sound heard close to the Hanging Tower. It is thought to be the death rattle of the young man who had deceived Marion. Although the White Lady of Ludlow Castle has not been glimpsed in recent years, there are still reports of this curious sound suggesting the agony of violent death.

The doomed hero of Warkworth Castle on the River Coquet, south-east of Alnwick, was Bertram of Bothal who owed fealty to the Lord Percy of Alnwick known in history as Hotspur. Before leading an attack on his long-standing enemy Earl Douglas, Hotspur held a banquet at Alnwick Castle. To it was invited the lord of Widdrington and his beautiful daughter Isabel who looked with a fond eye on handsome young Bertram.

During the festivities a minstrel sang of adventurous knights and chivalrous deeds, and Isabel, excited by his brave stories, later sent her maid to Sir Bertram bearing a helmet with a golden crest. The message was plain — when he had won the right to this helmet through deeds of valour, such as the troubadour described, she would marry him.

Soon Bertram had the opportunity to prove himself. Hotspur's forces crossed the Border and clashed with Douglas's Scots. His head full of Isabel and the gold-crested helmet, Bertram plunged into the thick of the battle and was badly wounded. When the mauled raiders withdrew, the injured knight was tied to a horse and taken to the castle of Wark on the Tweed to recover. Here he impatiently waited the arrival of his lady — her father had seen the affray and had promised that he would report the young knight's gallantry to Isabel and allow her to travel to Wark to nurse him.

After several days had passed and there was no sign of her, Bertram left his sickbed and journeyed with his brother to Widdrington to find out what had become of Lady Isabel. They reached her father's tower at dusk. It was ominously deserted.

At length an old woman, once Isabel's nurse, appeared and explained that six days ago her mistress had set out for Wark Castle. Realising that she must have come to harm on the way, Bertram disguised himself as a minstrel and went north in search of her. His brother set off in a different direction.

Several days later the despondent young man was resting beneath a hawthorn tree when a friar came by and was struck by the melancholy expression on his face. According to an old Border ballad he said:

> 'All minstrels yet that e'er I saw,
>  Are full of game and glee,
>  But thou art sad and woebegone;
>  I marvel whence it be.'

Sir Bertram explained his quest, hoping that the wandering monk might have news of his lost Isabel. The friar replied,

> 'Behind yon hills so steep and high,
>  Down in a lonely glen,
>  There stands a castle fair and strong,
>  Far from the abode of men.'

He added that when he had been passing this castle he had heard the voice of a girl crying at a turret window.

Bertram hurried to the castle and kept watch on it from a nearby cave.

On the second night, when a moonbeam played on the turret the friar had described, he saw the face of Isabel at an embrasure. He spent the next day in his cave trying to think of a way to rescue her.

On the third night weariness overtook him and he slept until dawn, then he opened his eyes and to his

136

dismay saw Isabel leaving the turret by means of a rope ladder. Holding it steady by the castle wall was a young man in the costume of a Scot. Aghast that Isabel could play him false with this youth, Bertram followed the couple until they were out of sight of the castle. Then, drawing the sword which he had secreted beneath his minstrel's cloak, he rushed at the Scot with the words, 'Yield that lady up or die.'

The young man drew his claymore and the clash of steel was accompanied by Isabel's anguished cries. A moment later the Scot was on the ground and, as the knight prepared to give him his death blow, the girl threw herself over his prostrate body.

'Stop, 'tis thy brother,' she cried.

Her words came too late.

The sweep of the blade could not be halted. As death began to glaze her eyes she managed to whisper to Sir Bertram how his brother, disguised as a Scot, had found her the captive of an outlaw and had arranged her escape.

Soon afterwards a band of searchers from the castle found the stunned figure of the English knight, standing dumbly by the bodies of his sweetheart and his brother, and took him prisoner.

Hotspur ransomed Bertram from his captors and sent him to his castle at Warkworth to get over the tragedy. But the mourning knight never did. He sold his gold-crested helmet and his possessions to benefit the poor, then quit Warkworth for a spot on the banks of the nearby Coquet. Here in the cliffs above the river he hewed out a hermit's cell and a little chapel where he could meditate and pray for the souls of those he had killed. Over the arch of the chapel he carved the words: 'My tears have been my meat day and night.'

Sir Bertram, now known as the Hermit of Warkworth, spent the rest of his life there, and after his death his sorrowing spectre has been seen standing by the Coquet close to the hermitage.

## Chapter 17

## Phantoms of the Border

The wild borderland between England and Scotland has the greatest concentration of haunted castles in the country. This is to be expected because no other part of Britain has had so much blood spilled on its soil. It is divided by the line of the Roman Wall which was built on the orders of the Emperor Hadrian to keep out the Picts. Begun in about AD 120, it stretched from coast to coast when completed. For the next two and a half centuries Roman soldiers manned it, shivering in the bitter winds and cursing the misty rain which gave cover to their enemies. After the Romans came the Saxons, who forced the British Celts into Wales and Scotland – but for a thousand years the Scots had their revenge by raiding over the abandoned wall to slaughter their traditional foes, burn down their churches and rustle their cattle.

To check these raiders – known as 'reivers' – the Norman kings encouraged their border barons to build castles to act as a buffer between their kingdom and the Scots. Often built with stones taken from the Roman Wall, many of these castles were 'pele towers' which were used as places of refuge for the local people until the danger had passed.

With generations of fighting behind them, these powerful border families feuded among themselves when they were not battling with the Scots, and there was no shortage of daring deeds and foul treachery to populate their castles with ghosts. Many of these castles are still standing and they have an air of toughness about them, unlike so many of the southern castles which became stately homes. Stand on their ramparts and gaze northwards over the unspoiled landscape and it is easy to believe the grim legends which have grown about them.

Let us make a tour of them, travelling east from Carlisle across to Newcastle, and starting with Carlisle Castle itself. William Rufus, the son of William the Conqueror, built it in 1092, and during its eventful history it was the home of Andrew Harcla, Earl of Carlisle, who was executed on account of his alliance with Robert the Bruce. Mary Queen of Scots began her long years of English imprisonment here, and during the Civil War Sir Thomas Glenham held it for the king, only surrendering to a Scots army when his besieged garrison was reduced to surviving on rats, linseed meal and dogs.

In 1745 it fell to the Jacobites but after the defeat of the rebels at Culloden many Scots were imprisoned within its walls and their cells are still to be seen.

Alterations were made to the castle in 1835 when a huge parade ground and barracks were built, and it was during this demolition and reconstruction that the skeleton of a lady was discovered bricked into the wall of the second story of the keep. She was dressed in silk tartan, there were valuable rings on her fingers and her feet rested on silk kerchiefs. No one could guess her identity or why her body had been sealed in, though there was great speculation as to whether she had been walled up alive.

It was probably her phantom which was seen by a soldier of the 93rd Regiment stationed at the castle in 1842. He was on guard duty in the precincts of the keep when he challenged an approaching figure. Receiving no reply, the sentry advanced upon it, shouting to rouse the guard as he did so. When he reached the figure it faded in

139

front of his eyes, and he collapsed with shock. He was found unconscious with his bayonet still sticking in the wall after an ineffectual lunge. He died several hours later.

The scene of one of Britain's most famous hauntings is Corby Castle which stands on the east bank of the River Eden east of Carlisle. The ghost is known as the Radiant Boy, and according to tradition to see him means a rise to fame and fortune — followed by a violent death.

The boy became a model for writers of ghostly stories after an account of him was published in Victorian times by Catherine Crowe. In *The Night Side of Nature* she explained how she had visited Corby Castle and had been shown a journal kept by one of the members of the family. She copied out the entry for 3 September 1803 in which the writer explained that among the guests staying at the castle was the Rector of Greystoke, referred to as Mr A—. The account read:

. . . they were to have remained with us some days, but their visit was cut short in a very unexpected manner. On the morning after their arrival we were all assembled at breakfast, when a chaise-and-four dashed up to the door in such haste that it knocked down part of the fence of my flower-garden. Our curiosity was, of course, awakened to know who could be arriving at so early an hour, when, happening to turn my eyes towards Mr A—, I observed that he appeared extremely agitated.

'It is our carriage,' said he. 'I am very sorry, but we must absolutely leave you this morning.'

We naturally felt, and expressed, considerable surprise, as well as regret, at this unexpected departure, representing that we had invited Colonel and Mrs S—, some friends whom Mr A— particularly desired to meet, to dine with us on that day. Our expostulations, however, were in vain; the breakfast was no sooner over than they departed, leaving us in consternation to conjecture what could possibly have occasioned so sudden an alteration in their arrangements.

It was some time later that the real reason came to light for the mysterious departure. The diarist visited the home of Mr A— who gave the following explanation:

Soon after we went to bed we fell asleep. It might be between one and two in the morning when I awoke. I observed that the fire was totally extinguished; but although that was the case, and we had no light, I saw a glimmer in the middle of the room, which suddenly increased to a bright flame. I looked out, apprehending that something had caught fire; when, to my amazement, I beheld a beautiful boy clothed in white, with bright locks, resembling gold, standing by my bedside, in which position he remained some minutes, fixing his eyes upon me with a mild and benevolent expression. He then glided gently towards the side of the chimney, where it is obvious there is no possible egress, and entirely disappeared. I found myself again in total darkness, and all remained quiet until the usual hour of rising. I declare this to be a true account of what I saw at Corby Castle, upon my word as a clergyman.

'The riders of Featherstone are abroad tonight,' Border folk used to say when the darkness was rent by terrified barking. They were referring to a wild band of ghosts known as the Phantom Hunt which from time to time struck midnight terror into the dogs of the neighbourhood.

The hunt always ended at Featherstone Castle which stands in parkland south-west of Haltwhistle on a beautiful stretch of the South Tyne. The oldest part of the castle dates back to 1212 when Helios de Featherstonehaugh was master of the estate. Its fourteenth-century pele tower had been added to with battlemented walls and watchtowers, making it one of the most picturesque castles in the area.

The legend of the Phantom Hunt began when Abigail, the beautiful only child of the last Baron Featherstone-haugh, fell in love with young Ridley of Hard Riding, an unfortunate choice as her father was determined she should marry a distant relative to cement a Border alliance.

After the reluctant girl had submitted to the cere-mony, the wedding party decided to go off on a hunt. Only the old baron — who had celebrated the success of his plan with too much wine — and his wife remained in the castle hall.

Away to the north streamed the riders to where a graceful bridge spanned the river with a flying arch — as it still does today. After urging their horses over it, they rode to a gloomy wood called Pynkinscleugh where they hoped to find deer. Instead they looked up to the high ground to see the grim figure of Ridley at the head of his armed retainers.

'Give up the Lady Abigail,' he demanded, 'or I shall bear her away over your corpses.'

'No Ridley shall take my bride!' retorted the bride-groom.

Drawing his sword, Ridley spurred his horse and charged through the snapping undergrowth at the sur-prised party and, while the vassals from Hard Riding and the vassals from Featherstone took each other's lives, he fought the bridegroom in single combat.

The Lady Abigail, distraught at the sight of her lover and her new husband slashing at each other with their broadswords, rushed between them — and was killed. The men continued to fight over her body until both were mortally wounded. Ridley collapsed over a bowl-shaped rock into which the blood flowed from his terrible wounds. As silence followed the clash of steel and the hoarse cries of the combatants, ravens of ill omen gathered round this rock and dipped their beaks

142

into the still-warm blood, thus giving it the name of the Ravens' Rock which it bears to this day.

Back at Featherstone Castle the baron woke at midnight and, by flickering torchlight, gazed over the tables with their empty wine goblets and platters of discarded food from the wedding feast. His wife dozed in her chair beside him. Suddenly the old man hauled himself to his feet to greet his guests as they walked silently through the doorway of the hall. Then to his horror he saw that each was disfigured with gaping wounds, each face had the pallor of death, and all moved through the furniture as though it did not exist.

Automatically he crossed himself and the ghastly company faded away. According to legend the baron went insane with the realisation that his daughter and the entire bridal party had returned as ghosts. The Phantom Hunt was believed to re-enact its return to Featherstone Castle from Pynkinscleugh at midnight on each anniversary of the ambush.

Featherstone Castle boasts two other ghosts. One is that of Sir Reginald FitzUrse who, as a prisoner in the old tower, was starved to death and whose groans are occasionally heard as a reminder of his agony long ago. The other is the mysterious Green Lady who is still seen.

'One day I saw a strange woman walking down a corridor,' Jane Butcher, who comes from the Wallace family which owned the castle, told me. 'She was wearing a dress or gown of a greeny-brown colour – and she seemed to be a real person. Not knowing who she was, I followed her down the passage where she went into a room at the end of it. I knew I would find her in there because there is absolutely no other exit – not even a window. But when I went into the room it was empty, and I knew then that I had seen the Green Lady.'

Other people who have lived or worked at the castle have reported exactly the same happening as described by Jane.

*

The Grey Man of Bellister is still seen where he was murdered in the grounds of a castle on the bank of the South Tyne near Haltwhistle. It stands on a high mound, once encircled by a moat, and consists of a square squat tower to which a Victorian house has been added.

A Border ballad describes the violent death of an old minstrel at the thirteenth-century tower which gave rise to the ghost story.

> O Bellister stands pleasantlie
> Beside the bonny Tyne;
> But wi' a deed of crueltie
> Is wedded to lang syne.

The minstrel was an old man who travelled from hall to hall with his harp, providing an evening's entertainment for his night's food and lodging. He particularly liked singing his ballads at Bellister, but in those days of Scottish raiding parties and Border feuds suspicion was never far from anyone's mind, and it occurred to the harsh lord of Bellister that the minstrel's frequent visits could mean that he was a spy.

When the old man departed one morning with his harp slung over his shoulder, the master of the castle ordered his fierce bloodhounds to be released. As soon as he heard their deep baying the old minstrel began to run for the river, but the pack overtook him as he reached the bank and savaged him to death. Since then his grey form has restlessly haunted the tower.

Another version of the legend is that the minstrel was not killed by the Bellister bloodhounds but, like other victims, was hanged from the lowest branch of the great sycamore which overshadows the castle.

A man who believes he has seen the Grey Man recently is David Hunter, of Haltwhistle, who gave me the following account:

It was a very bright moon with just a slight trace of a

haze around it and I could discern quite a bit of detail in the hedgerows and landscape.

I'd been walking with my dogs for ten minutes or so and had stopped on a small bridge over the Tippalt burn to charge my pipe and watch for rising trout as I usually did at this point. When I'd got my pipe drawing to my satisfaction I prepared to continue on my walk and noticed the dogs were staring very fixedly at a point some fifty or sixty yards away over the field. I noticed they seemed very frightened of something so I looked in the direction they were staring and saw someone walking over the field towards the river South Tyne which is joined by the Tippalt burn just below the bridge. He was approaching a fence at the end of the field and just beyond the fence the ground fell away where the river had washed out the topsoil over the years until now there was a drop of about six or seven feet on to the riverside stones. To my amazement, when he got to the fence, instead of climbing over it as I expected him to, he just walked on as though there was no fence there at all.

This made me very curious and I watched him very closely and noticed that he was very oddly dressed by present-day standards, and he was carrying some kind of pack like a bundle of rags or clothes and a rather strange stringed instrument, like an ancient banjo or guitar the type of which I'd never seen before.

Now came the time when my curiosity changed to fear as he reached the edge of the field and just carried on walking six or more feet above the stones towards the site of an old ford on what use to be the road into Haltwhistle. It was also the direct route to Bellister Castle. I don't remember how long I stood there petrified by fear but eventually I was able to move again and this I did with a speed I never found either before or since.

Never again will I mock anyone I hear talking about ghosts or the supernatural since I saw one with my own eyes – a disbeliever was well and truly converted that night.

Death by mistake has left eerie echoes in Haughton Castle – ghostly screams which were only quietened by an old Bible. The castle, whose windows gaze across the North Tyne near Chollerton, once belonged to Sir John de Widdrington. At that time the Border was a lawless place, made worse by the fact that Lord Dacre of Gilsland had been appointed Lord Warden of the Marches. Instead of pacifying the area, he was known to be in league with freebooting families who preyed on their neighbours. The oppressed locals asked Sir John to travel to York to inform Cardinal Wolsey of the unhappy situation.

Just before he was about to begin his journey Sir John's followers captured an outlaw named Archie Armstrong. He was thrown into a dungeon and Sir John, his head full of the importance of his mission, rode out. It was only when he reached York that he found the key of the dungeon in his pocket. He realised with a thrill of horror the plight of the prisoner, for it was the only key in existence which could unlock the dungeon door.

He immediately began the return journey, galloping so fast that by the time he reached Durham one horse had died beneath him. When he finally arrived at the castle his first words were to ask about the prisoner. The retainers answered that for the first two days they had heard a lot of shouting from behind the thick oaken door but latterly there had been silence.

Sir John ran to the door, turned the key in the lock – and found Archie Armstrong sprawled on the floor, dead from thirst.

As a protest at his untimely end the phantom of the outlaw returned to Haughton Castle, and his despairing cries rang again and again from the dungeon to torment the inhabitants and drive away the servants. A minister was called to exorcise the spirit and the ceremony appeared to be successful though the Bible which had been used was kept at the castle as a protection against the spirit's return.

Years later it was found that the leather binding of the book was crumbling and it was dispatched to London for rebinding. Almost immediately after it had gone the dying screams of Archie Armstrong were heard again in the castle. A messenger was sent to London to bring back the book, after which peace was restored.

A very similar legend belongs to Spedlin's Tower in Dumfries and Galloway Region. During the reign of Charles II Sir Alexander Jardine had a miller named Porteous arrested on the charge of trying to burn down his own mill. The reason for this strange behaviour is not recorded but we do know that the miller was imprisoned in a dungeon beneath the tower. Soon afterwards Sir Alexander received an urgent message requiring him to go to Edinburgh. It was not until he reached that city and was passing the city prison that he remembered to his horror that he carried the only key to the Spedlin dungeon in his pocket.

He sent a messenger galloping back to the tower with the key, but in the meantime the miller had died of starvation. But if the heavy door of the dungeon had been too thick for Porteous's cries to reach the inhabitants of the castle, it was no barrier for the ghost. Day and night he revenged himself on the Jardines with every conceivable poltergeist trick.

Finally it was a service of exorcism which drove the frantic spirit back into the dungeon, and a Bible, which had been used in the service, was placed in a niche in the stairwell leading down to the cell to keep Porteous from returning to annoy the family.

The Bible could not muffle the dead miller's voice, and often a scream would ring through the tower, followed by the words, 'Let me out, let me out, I am dying of hunger.'

Sometimes someone more daring than the rest would

creep down the stairs to the dungeon and, by putting an ear to the iron-studded door, would hear the sound of Porteous cursing the family and the scratching of his fingers. If a twig was stuck through the keyhole the famished ghost would scrape off the bark.

In the course of time the Jardine family moved to a new mansion, known as Jardine Hall, which stood on the other side of the River Annan, but the Bible was left in its niche to contain the angry spirit.

Askerton Castle near Brampton, whose twin battlemented towers are now surrounded by farm buildings, is haunted by a White Lady who was mentioned in a Border ballad:

> Hard by the Castle Askerton
> Lived bonnie May Marye;
> The bonnicst lass, I wol, was she
> In a' the north countrie.

Bonnie May Marye was murdered by a rejected lover at a spot called Yellow Coat Slack, and it is her white phantom which appears in the grounds round Askerton. A legend says that she once halted a horseman by laying hold of his bridle, with the result that the horse was paralysed until the rider had made a promise which, if he repeated it, would result in his death. Then the ghost melted away.

The phantom of Lady Derwentwater haunts the ruins of Dilston Castle near Corbridge. She is waiting for her husband James who will never return. Sometimes her lamp, as spectral as herself, shines as a beacon from a high paneless window where in happier days she used to watch for his coming. He was beheaded on Tower Hill in 1716 for his part in the Jacobite rebellion against George I.

In complete contrast to ruined Dilston, Langley Castle near Haydon Bridge is famous for its medieval banquets and 'Dracula night' entertainments for tourists and holiday-makers, but it really is haunted — by a spectral coach driven by a headless driver.

Naworth Castle near Brampton has another female ghost. Legend tells that a Lord Dacre of Naworth jilted a local girl in order to marry a lady of his own rank. The rejected girl drowned herself in a stream flowing by the castle on the night of the marriage.

The next morning Lord Dacre walked out with his new wife and found the girl in the water. At the same time her mother, who had been searching desperately for her daughter through the night, came upon the scene. Blaming Lord Dacre for her daughter's tragedy, she cried out a curse which, rather remarkably considering the circumstances, was in rhyme:

> 'O curst be the cruel hand
> That wrought this hour to me!
> May evil grim aye follow him
> Until the day he dee.'

Lord Dacre did not live very long after that. Three years after his death, in 1577, his only legitimate son fell from a rocking horse so that, according to a chronicler, 'he had the brains bruised out of his head', and thus the male line of the Dacres died out.

Though the girl was revenged, her spirit is still said to haunt the spot by the castle where she died.

One more ghostly Border lady deserves a mention, the Grey Lady of Prudhoe Castle, who is reputed to glide along its passages at night. It was said that she had some connection with a secret tunnel which was supposed to run from Purdhoe to Bywell Castle several miles to the west, but now the passage is as much a mystery as the pale ghost.

# Haunted castles for you to see

Most of the castles described in this book are open to the public, but some private castles have such good stories that they have been included. A good view of these private castles can usually be obtained from nearby roads, especially in the Border country. A large-scale map is very useful for locating the castles and their best vantage points, but please respect the privacy of people living in them — it should not be forgotten that an Englishman's castle is often his home.

Some owners of private castles allow enthusiasts to make special visits if a letter is sent beforehand.

The Department of the Environment has quite a few castles in its care. Ruins which do not need a permanent custodian may be visited at any reasonable time, the other castles have standard hours of entry in England and Wales:

|                      | Weekdays     | Sundays  |
|----------------------|--------------|----------|
| March to April       | 9.30–5.30    | 2–5.30   |
| May to September     | 9.30–7       | 2–7      |
| October              | 9.30–5.30    | 2–5.30   |
| November to February | 9.30–4       | 2–4      |

Standard hours of entry in Scotland are:

|                      | Weekdays     | Sundays  |
|----------------------|--------------|----------|
| April to September   | 9.30–7       | 2–7      |
| October to March     | 9.30–4       | 2–4      |

Like most privately owned castles, those under the care of the Department of the Environment are closed on Christmas Eve, Christmas Day and Boxing Day in England and Wales. In Scotland they are closed on Christmas Day and New Year's Day.

From season to season castle opening times may be altered, so to avoid disappointment it is wise to check the details before you make your visit. The annual publication *Historic Houses, Castles & Gardens* is useful for its up-to-date information. The list on pages 155–9 gives castle locations and an indication of when they are open to the public.

To get a rough idea of where a castle is you can use the maps on pages 152–4. Look the castle up on the list on pages 155–9 and note the map reference. Turn to whichever map is mentioned – A, B or C – and look for the number. The castles are numbered alphabetically so if you want to find out what castle a number on a map refers to look down the list for the letter of the map and the number – 33 on Map A, for example, will be near the end of the list because it is a high number.

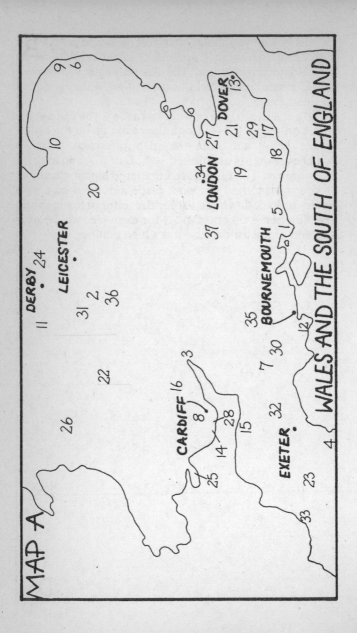

MAP A

WALES AND THE SOUTH OF ENGLAND

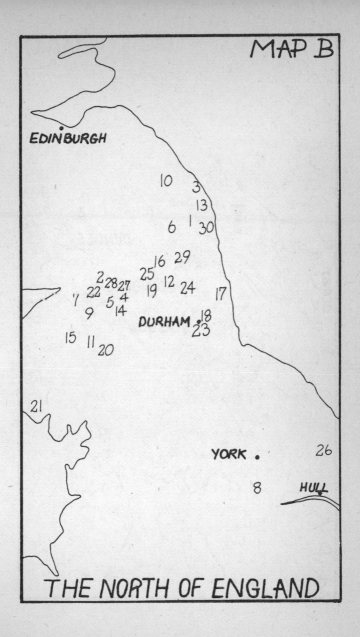

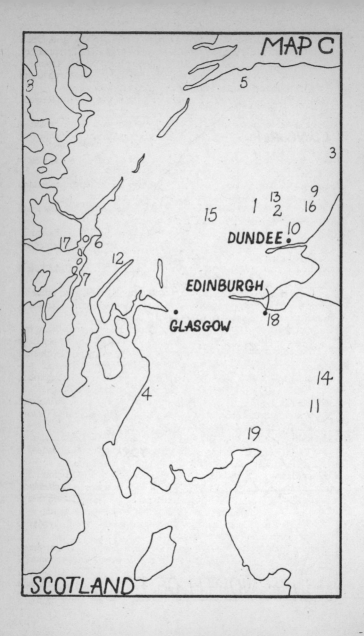

MAP C

SCOTLAND

**Alnwick Castle** *(pages 35–6)*   At Alnwick in Northumberland. Open afternoons (except Saturday) from early May to late September.

**Arundel Castle** *(pages 68–70)*   At Arundel in West Sussex. Open afternoons (except Saturday and Sunday) from end March to end October and Sunday afternoons during summer season.

**Ashintully Castle** *(pages 88–9)*   Near Kirkmichael in Tayside Region. Private property.

**Askerton Castle** *(page 148)*   Now part of a farm by the road which runs north from Brampton to Shopford in Cumbria. Private property.

**Astley Castle** *(page 14)*   On the B4102 about 6 km (3¾ miles) west of Nuneaton in Warwickshire. Now a hotel.

**Bamburgh Castle** *(pages 76–9)*   At Bamburgh on the Northumberland coast. Open afternoons from Easter to end October.

**Bellister Castle** *(pages 144–6)*   Overlooking the South Tyne just south of Haltwhistle in Northumberland. Private property.

**Berkeley Castle** *(pages 50–51)*   South of Berkeley in Gloucestershire. Open afternoons (except Monday) from 1 April to end September and Sunday afternoons during October.

**Berry Pomeroy Castle** *(pages 16–23)*   Off the A385 which links Totnes and Paignton in Devon. Open daily.

**Blenkinsopp Castle** *(pages 128–30)*   Stands on a knoll south of the A69 between Greenhead and Haltwhistle in Cumbria. Now a club and caravan park.

**Bramber Castle** *(pages 113–4)*   In the care of the National Trust, its ruins are situated at Bramber village in West Sussex. Open daily (except Monday and Saturday) from Good Friday to October.

**Burgh Castle** *(page 112)*   At the meeting place of the Yare and Waveney rivers, 5 km (3 miles) south-west of Great Yarmouth in Norfolk. Department of the Environment standard hours.

**Cadbury Castle** *(pages 56–7)*   South of the A303 between Wincanton and Sparkford in Somerset. The earthworks are open to visitors at any reasonable time.

**Caerphilly Castle** *(pages 74–5)*   At Caerphilly in Mid Glamorgan. Department of the Environment standard hours. The castle is also open Sunday mornings from April to September.

**Caister Castle** *(pages 67–8)*   Close to Caister-on-Sea in Norfolk. Open daily (except Saturday) from mid-May to end September.

**Callaly Castle** *(pages 84–5)*   Situated west of the A697, 14 km (8¾ miles) west of Alnwick in Northumberland. Open Saturday, Sunday and Bank Holiday Monday afternoons from early May to late September.

**Carlisle Castle** *(pages 139–40)*   At Carlisle in Cumbria. Department of the Environment standard hours. Also open Sunday mornings from April to September.

**Castle Rising** *(page 52)*   About 6 km (3¾ miles) north-east of King's Lynn in Norfolk. Department of the Environment standard hours. The castle is also open Sunday mornings from April to September.

**Cawood Castle** *(pages 114–17)* At Cawood, 6 km (3¾ miles) north-west of Selby in North Yorkshire. Private property.

**Chartley Castle** *(page 68)* Its ruins stand on private property close to the A518 between Uttoxeter and Stafford in Staffordshire.

**Corby Castle** *(pages 140–41)* Close to Great Corby, about 6 km (3¾ miles) east of Carlisle in Cumbria. The grounds only are open on Thursdays.

**Corfe Castle** *(pages 46–9)* Overlooking the village of the same name in Dorset. Open daily all year.

**Cortachy Castle** *(pages 96–8)* Just north of Kirriemuir in Tayside Region. Private property.

**Coupland Castle** *(page 84)* About 6 km (3¾ miles) north-west of Wooler in Northumberland. Private property.

**Crathes Castle** *(page 6)* About 22 km (13½ miles) south-west of Aberdeen. Open afternoons from 1 May to end September.

**Culzean Castle** *(pages 95–6)* Near Maybole, Strathclyde Region. Open daily from 1 April to end October. Grounds always open.

**Dacre Castle** *(pages 52–4)* Close to Dacre village, just north of Ullswater in Cumbria. Private property.

**Dilston Castle** *(page 148)* South of the A69 between Hexham and Corbridge in Northumberland. On private property but permission to visit the ruins may be obtained at the office.

**Dover Castle** *(pages 101–2)* At Dover in Kent. Department of the Environment standard hours. The castle is also open Sunday mornings from April to September.

**Dunphail Castle** *(page 6)* About 11 km (6¾ miles) south of Forres in Grampian Region. Private property.

**Dunraven Castle** *(pages 106–7)* Just south of Southerndown in Mid Glamorgan. Private property.

**Dunstaffnage Castle** *(page 73)* Overlooking Loch Etive 5 km (3 miles) north-east of Oban. Open all year round but closing at 4 during the winter.

**Dunstanburgh Castle** *(pages 59–61)* In the care of the National Trust, the castle is 2 km (1¼ miles) north of Craster on the Northumberland coast. Department of the Environment hours.

**Dunster Castle** *(pages 109–10)* At Dunster in Somerset. In the care of the National Trust, the castle is open daily (except Friday and Saturday) from early April to end September. Open in October on Tuesday, Wednesday and Sunday afternoons.

**Duntrune Castle** *(pages 94–5)* On the coast west of the A816, about 12 km (7½ miles) north-west of Lochgilphead in Strathclyde Region. Private property.

**Dunvegan Castle** *(page 74)* In the north-west of the Isle of Skye. Open daily (except Sunday) at varying times from early April to late October.

**Edzell Castle** *(pages 86–8)*   Close to Edzell village, 9 km (5½ miles) north of Brechin in Tayside Region. Department of the Environment standard hours.

**Featherstone Castle** *(pages 141–3)*   Standing in parkland on the bank of the South Tyne 5 km (3 miles) south-west of Haltwhistle in Cumbria. Privately owned.

**Glamis Castle** *(pages 37–45)*   Stands off the A94 between Forfar and the village of Glamis in Tayside Region. Open at Easter weekend, and afternoons (except Saturday) from 1 May to end September.

**Goodrich Castle** *(pages 131–2)*   Near Goodrich village south of Ross-on-Wye in Hereford and Worcester. Department of the Environment standard hours.

**Greystoke Castle** *(page 108)*   Just off the B5288 west of Penrith in Cumbria. Private property.

**Hastings Castle** *(pages 80–81)*   Overlooking Hastings in East Sussex. Open during the summer.

**Haughton Castle** *(pages 146–7)*   Off the B6320 overlooking the North Tyne between Chollerton and Wark. Private property.

**Hermitage Castle** *(pages 30–35)*   Close to Hermitage village 20 km (12½ miles) south of Hawick in Borders Region. Department of the Environment standard hours.

**Herstmonceux Castle** *(pages 98–101)*   Just south of Herstmonceux village near Eastbourne in East Sussex. Only the castle's grounds are open Monday to Friday afternoons from 1 April to end Oct.

**Hever Castle** *(pages 49–50)*   At Hever near Edenbridge in Kent. Open on Tuesday, Wednesday, Friday, Sunday and Bank Holiday Monday afternoons from Easter Sunday to late September.

**Hylton Castle** *(pages 91–3)*   Just outside Sunderland in Tyne and Wear. Open daily (afternoon only on Sunday).

**Inveraray Castle** *(pages 62–4)*   At Inveraray in Argyll, Strathclyde Region. Open mornings and afternoons (except Sunday morning and Friday) from early April to end June and September; all day (except Sunday morning) in July and August.

**Inverquharity Castle** *(page 88)*   Situated on private property about 5 km (3 miles) north of Kirriemuir in Tayside Region.

**Jedburgh Castle** *(pages 104–6)*   At Jedburgh in Borders Region. Open weekday mornings and afternoons, and on Saturday and Sunday afternoons.

**Kimbolton Castle** *(page 50)*   On the A45 12 km (7½ miles) north-west of St Neots in Cambridgeshire. Open on Bank Holidays and on Sunday afternoons from mid-July to end August.

**Lambton Castle** *(pages 89–91)*   About 2 km (1¼ miles) north-east of Chester-le-Street in Durham. On private ground, the original castle was replaced by a hall in the eighteenth century and is now a school.

**Langley Castle** *(pages 148–9)*   On the A686 2 km (1¼ miles) south-west of Haydon Bridge in Northumberland. Now used as a banqueting hall.

**Leeds Castle** *(page 68)*   Off the A20 about 7 km (4¼ miles) east of Maidstone in Kent. Open Tuesday, Wednesday, Thursday, Sunday and Bank Holiday Monday afternoons from 1 April to end October and every afternoon in August.

**Lowther Castle** *(pages 110–12)*   Situated close to the A6, about 6 km (3¾ miles) south of Penrith, on a side road running west to Askham in Cumbria. Private property.

**Ludlow Castle** *(pages 134–5)*   At Ludlow in Salop. Open mornings and afternoons 1 April to 30 September, weekdays only from 1 October to 31 March.

**Lydford Castle** *(page 83)*   At Lydford, about 12 km (7½ miles) north of Tavistock in Devon. In the care of the Department of the Environment, it can be visited at any reasonable time.

**Meggernie Castle** *(pages 121–3)*   In Glen Lyon off the A827 30 km (18½ miles) west of Aberfeldy in Tayside. Private property.

**Melgund Castle** *(page 106)*   About 7 km (4¼ miles) south-west of Brechin in Tayside Region. Private property.

**Moy Castle** *(pages 71–3)*   By Loch Buie on the south coast of the Isle of Mull. Private property.

**Muncaster Castle** *(page 54)*   On the A595 close to Ravenglass in Cumbria. Open Tuesday, Wednesday, Thursday and Sunday afternoons from Easter Saturday to early October.

**Naworth Castle** *(page 149)*   On private property, it can be seen from the road which crosses the park from Lanercost Priory to the A69 near Brampton in Cumbria.

**Neville's Castle** *(page 83)*   To the west of Durham in County Durham. Private property.

**Nottingham Castle** *(pages 51–2)*   At Nottingham. Open weekdays and Sunday afternoons all year.

**Pennard Castle** *(page 75)*   Above Three Cliffs Bay south-west of Swansea in West Glamorgan. Open at any reasonable time.

**Powis Castle** *(pages 124–7)*   In the care of the National Trust, the castle is on a knoll close to Welshpool in Powys. Open afternoons (except Monday and Tuesday) from mid-April to end September.

**Prudhoe Castle** *(page 149)*   The ruins stand near Prudhoe village in Northumberland. They are in the care of the Department of the Environment and the public are admitted at certain times. It is best to check locally.

**Rochester Castle** *(pages 132–4)*   At Rochester in Kent. DoE hours.

**Rosslyn Castle** *(pages 64–5)*   At Roslin village near the A6094, about 12 km (7½ miles) south of Edinburgh. Private property but the public are admitted to the ruins at certain times. The Rosslyn chapel is always open.

**St Donat's Castle** *(page 103)*   Near Llantwit Major 12 km (7½ miles) south of Bridgend in South Glamorgan. Private property.

**Scotney Castle** *(page 108)*   In the care of the National Trust, the castle is on the A21 about 1 km (½ mile) south of Lamberhurst in Kent. Gardens surrounding the castle are open afternoons (except Monday and Tuesday) from 1 April to end October.

**Sewingshields Castle** *(pages 57–9)* North of the Roman Wall by the B6318 in the Sewingshields Crags area, about 7 km (4¼ miles) north of Haydon Bridge in Northumberland. The remaining mounds and ditches can be visited at any reasonable time.

**Sherborne Castle** *(page 93)* To the east of Sherborne in Dorset. Department of the Environment standard hours.

**Skipsea Castle** *(pages 117–9)* Its mounds are on Albermarle Hill between Bridlington and Hornsea in Humberside. In the care of the Department of the Environment, it can be visited at any reasonable time.

**Spedlin's Tower** *(pages 147–8)* On the south-west bank of the River Annan about 5 km (3 miles) north of Lochmaben in Dumfries and Galloway Region. Private property.

**Tamworth Castle** *(page 83)* At Tamworth in Staffordshire. Open weekdays (except Fridays from October to February) and Sunday afternoons all year.

**Taunton Castle** *(pages 81–3)* At Taunton in Somerset. Part of the building is the Castle Hotel, the remainder a museum and library which is open daily from 10 to 4 (except Sunday).

**Thirlwall Castle** *(pages 127–8)* Near the village of Greenhead on the A69 in Northumberland. Private property but permission to visit may be obtained at the nearby farm.

**Tintagel Castle** *(page 56)* At Tintagel in Cornwall. Department of the Environment standard hours. The castle is also open Sunday mornings from April to September.

**Tower of London** *(pages 7–15)* Open weekdays all year and Sunday afternoons from 1 March to end October.

**Triermain Castle** *(pages 65–7)* Also known as Gilsland Castle, its ruined tower is situated in a farmer's field by the B6318 4 km (2½ miles) west of Gilsland in Cumbria.

**Wallington Hall** *(page 85)* Near Cambo, 17 km (10½ miles) west of Morpeth in Northumberland. Remains of the old castle are incorporated in it. In the care of the National Trust, it is open afternoons (except Tuesday) from mid-April to end September.

**Wardour Castle** *(page 70)* Situated in Wardour Park off the A30, 23 km (14¼ miles) west of Salisbury in Wiltshire. Open Monday, Wednesday, Friday and Saturday afternoons from late July to early September.

**Warkworth Castle** *(pages 135–7)* At Warkworth on the River Coquet in Northumberland. Department of the Environment standard hours.

**Warwick Castle** *(pages 120–21)* At Warwick in Warwickshire. Open daily.

**Windsor Castle** *(pages 24–9)* At Windsor in Berkshire. Castle precincts open daily.

# More Beaver Books

We hope you have enjoyed this Beaver Book. Here are some of the other titles:

**The Beaver Book of Horror Stories** A Beaver original. A spine-chilling collection for older readers by such master horror writers as Ray Bradbury and H. P. Lovecraft; edited, and with a specially-written contribution, by Mark Ronson

**Ghostly Laughter** A Beaver original. The chief characters in this unusual collection of stories are ghosts with a difference – they are so eccentric and lovable they will make you laugh! Chosen by Barbara Ireson, the stories are a hilarious and thrilling read for the nine-and-over age group

**Fantasy Tales** A collection of strange and wonderful stories – some frightening, some fantastic – which make enthralling reading for people of ten and over. Edited by Barbara Ireson

These and many other Beavers are available from your local bookshop or newsagent, or can be ordered direct from: Hamlyn Paperback Cash Sales, PO Box 11, Falmouth, Cornwall TR10 9EN. Send a cheque or postal order made payable to the Hamlyn Publishing Group, for the price of the book plus postage at the following rates:
UK: 45p for the first book, 20p for the second book, and 14p for each additional book ordered to a maximum charge of £1.63;
BFPO and Eire: 45p for the first book, 20p for the second book, plus 14p per copy for the next 7 books and thereafter 8p per book;
OVERSEAS: 75p for the first book and 21p for each extra book.

New Beavers are published every month and if you would like the *Beaver Bulletin*, a newsletter which tells you about new books and gives a complete list of titles and prices, send a large stamped addressed envelope to:

> **Beaver Bulletin**
> The Hamlyn Group
> Astronaut House
> Feltham
> Middlesex TW14 9AR

204812